WHAT PEOPLE ARE SAYING ABOUT KATIE J. TRENT AND *A MERRY AND BRIGHT ADVENTURE...*

Christmas can be a memorable and festive time for families, but it's all too easy to let shopping, decorating, and the general hustle and bustle take over so that we miss the true significance of the season. With her fun activities and meaningful devotional readings, Katie Trent is helping families embrace the wonder of Christ's birth each day of the Advent season.

—*Jim Daly*
President, Focus on the Family

I love this tool for teaching children about Christmas! *A Merry and Bright Adventure* is biblical, practical, and teaches about traditions along with God's Word. Parents will be blessed with this well-organized, spiritually sensitive resource for the Advent season. I highly recommend it to every family. Parents will learn some new things as well.

—*Dr. Scott Turansky*
Cofounder, National Center for Biblical Parenting

Katie has created a wonderful family Advent devotional with step-by-step guides to creating joyful memories together this Christmas!

—*Brock Eastman*
Author, *Saint Nicking at Night* and *Faith and Science with Dr. Fizzlebop*

When busyness calls our name during the Advent season, it can be difficult to keep Christ at the center of Christmas. Katie J. Trent does a fantastic job helping families refocus on the coming of Jesus through creative, flexible, and simple resources in her newest book *A Merry and Bright Adventure*. As a homeschool mom, I can confidently say parents will benefit from bringing these gospel-centered activities and devotionals into their homes as well as their hearts.

—*Becky Beresford*
Speaker, coach, and author, *She Believed HE Could, So She Did*

A Merry and Bright Adventure is a Christmas treasure your family will enjoy year after year. It is a wonderful guide for how to focus on the true meaning of Christmas and connect with your family in delightful and delicious ways!

—*Andrea Fortenberry*
Host, *The Perfectionist's Guide to Mothering* podcast

If your family is looking to grow closer to Christ and each other this holiday season, *A Merry and Bright Adventure* is exactly what you need. Katie J. Trent has put together a timeless devotional that helps remind us of the importance of gathering together around God's Word to deepen our faith through family, fun, and food! From nuggets found in God's Word and prayer to tasty treats, this devotional will surely add nostalgic memories to your family's Advent traditions.

—*Carlie Kercheval*
Hostess, Wives of Integrity Online Conference
and *Wives of Integrity podcast*

25 Days of Holiday Activities and Recipes for Families

A MERRY *and* BRIGHT
ADVENTURE

*A Christmas Devotional
for Family, Faith, Food, and Fun*

Author of *Recipes for a Sweet Child*
KATIE J. TRENT

A Merry and Bright Adventure
A Christmas Devotional for Family, Faith, Food, and Fun

katiejtrent.com

ISBN: 979-8-88769-276-0
eBook ISBN: 979-8-88769-279-1
Printed in Colombia
© 2024 by Katie J. Trent

Whitaker House
1030 Hunt Valley Circle
New Kensington, PA 15068
www.whitakerhouse.com

Library of Congress Cataloging-in-Publication Data
Names: Trent, Katie J., author.
Title: A merry and bright adventure : a Christmas devotional for family,
    faith, food, and fun / Katie J. Trent.
Description: New Kensington, PA : Whitaker House, [2024] | Summary:
    "Provides suggestions for Advent activities to assist families in
    preparing for Christmas as well as information on holiday traditions,
    prayers, Scripture readings, discussion questions, and recipes with
    full-color photos"— Provided by publisher.
Identifiers: LCCN 2024012216 (print) | LCCN 2024012217 (ebook) | ISBN
    9798887692760 | ISBN 9798887692791 (ebook)
Subjects: LCSH: Advent—Prayers and devotions. | Christmas—Prayers and
    devotions. | BISAC: RELIGION / Holidays / Christmas & Advent | RELIGION
    / Christian Living / Devotional
Classification: LCC BV40 .T73 2024 (print) | LCC BV40 (ebook) | DDC
    242/.33—dc23/eng/20240516
LC record available at https://lccn.loc.gov/2024012216
LC ebook record available at https://lccn.loc.gov/2024012217

1 2 3 4 5 6 7 8 9 10 11 ᚹ 31 30 29 28 27 26 25 24

DEDICATION

To our family and friends near and far:
Thank you for making an impact in our lives and being the hands
and feet of Jesus.

CONTENTS

ACKNOWLEDGMENTS

It is an incredible honor to have the opportunity to share my heart with readers around the world. I thank God for leading and guiding me every step of the way. I also want to thank my wonderful family. You're the reason I do what I do. Thank you for sacrificing time together, sharing your feedback, and enriching my life. I love and appreciate you more than you'll ever know.

Thank you to my mother, Kathy, who worked tirelessly to make the holidays such a special and meaningful time in our lives. I'll forever cherish the memories we made over the years, and we still carry on many of the traditions you started with us.

I also want to thank my agent, friend, and birthday buddy, Cheryl Ricker, and her husband Dwight. We love and appreciate you both. You've blessed our lives, and your prayers have been invaluable. I'm thankful we get to walk this journey of life together.

It's a joy to get to continue to work with the phenomenal team at Whitaker House. Thank you, Christine Whitaker, for believing in me and this project. Thank you, Peg Fallon, for your attention to detail and support throughout the process. And thank you to Amy Bartlett for bringing it all together and to Becky Speer for another gorgeous design! I truly appreciate every one of you and the ways you utilize your gifts and talents for the glory of God. It's a privilege to work alongside you.

I also want to give a special thanks to all of my *baking buddies* on this project. Thank you for testing out the recipes, offering feedback, and catching my errors: Aleene Belle Phillips, Carlie Kercheval, Cindy Variz, Crystal Hill, Erin Johnson, Gail Sowin, Heather Riddle, Jade Wilson, Jennifer Baldyga, Kristen Rattanamongkhoune, Lori Kelleher, Molly Cash, Richie Soares, Shirley Goertzen, Serena Wade-Harrington, and Tonya Sinner.

INTRODUCTION

The word Advent means "arrival" or "coming." We embrace Advent as a special time leading up to Christmas, a time to prepare our hearts and remember why Jesus came to earth for us.

The season begins the fourth Sunday before Christmas and includes all of the time leading up to that holy day. Many observe Advent by utilizing a wreath with four candles that are lit each Sunday—first one, then two, then three, and finally all four. Each week typically centers around a theme, such as hope, peace/preparation, joy, and love.

If your family has an Advent wreath, you'll notice this devotional correlates perfectly with those themes in its four sections. You could begin each new section of the book on Sunday along with your candle lighting. Alternatively, you could light the candle on Sunday and start the section on Monday because there are only six days of devotions in each section with the exception of the last one, which also includes a devotion for Christmas Day. Feel free to do whatever works best for your schedule.

Many families, including ours, have embraced the idea of observing Advent. Even though it wasn't something we were taught in our church, we liked the idea of being more intentional in keeping our focus on Jesus throughout the Christmas season. We've utilized a number of different countdowns, traditions, and devotionals over the years, so I have included the things our family loves most about the Advent season in *A Merry and Bright Adventure*.

Even if you don't participate in an Advent tradition, this devotional works beautifully as a December countdown to Christmas; it also allows you to be more intentional in discipleship while you meaningfully connect as a family throughout the holidays. You can start with chapter 1 on December 1 and go through one chapter each day, which will lead you all the way through to chapter 25 on Christmas Day. This is how our family typically enjoys the season together. And don't worry if you miss a day or can't get to all the activities—feel free to skip or combine them. The choice is yours. This will be a devotional you'll want to return to year after year, so be flexible. The most important thing is to have fun while focusing on the true meaning of Christmas.

Amid this commercialized holiday season, we all want to be more intentional in pointing our children to Jesus and remembering why we celebrate in the first place. This unique family devotional will help you discover new ways to enjoy the season's sights and sounds with Christ at the center of it all. You'll grow in your relationship with Jesus—and each other—as you learn to look at common holiday sights and sounds with a new perspective.

Every Advent, I love finding different ways to talk to my children about Jesus. We've done a variety of Advent activities over the years, but one of the most meaningful has been studying the history behind our holiday traditions and learning to see Christ in everyday items and moments.

Now, whenever we see common holiday objects—like stars, wreaths, or candy canes—we recall how they point us to Christ, and we take a moment to praise God together. The holidays become extra special when we ponder the sights, sounds, and smells in relation to how much God loves us. This transforms the mundane into the miraculous each and every day!

Before You Start

Here are a few things to help you prepare for your family *adventures* this year. First, the book is divided into four sections that correlate with the four weeks of Advent: hope, peace/preparation, joy, and love. Within these pages, you'll find more than enough lessons and activities to treasure, but you can always dive deeper too, especially if you have older children or want to incorporate this into homeschool lesson planning. (See the Homeschool *Adventure* Guide for ideas and suggestions.)

But before I dive into how to do more, allow me to invite you to do less! Christmastime is already a busy season to begin with. This book is designed to help you make it more meaningful and memorable, not more stressful and chaotic! Think of this devotional as an arsenal of tools for your toolbelt. Feel free to use those that are helpful each day and reserve the rest for another day—or even another year.

You will find *A Merry and Bright Adventure* loaded with ways to engage as a family. You definitely don't have to do all of the activities each day. Feel free to simply read the Scripture and devotion, then recite the prayer together. That is absolutely enough! Or you can choose to dive into the discussion, complete the family activity, and make the recipe. I have tried to include a variety of breakfast, lunch, snack, and beverage ideas to keep it super simple. There are also some recipe options so you can make whatever works best for your family. Feel free to utilize your own creative ideas too. You can always use the conversation connection section to tie in with something you're already making that day.

Chapter Organization

Each of the twenty-five chapters begins with a Scripture reading and focuses on a specific holiday tradition, followed by a prayer. There are discussion questions to kick off a family conversation and an adventure or activity to help you spend quality time together and reflect on the day's theme. Finally, there is a Baking Buddies Conversation Connection—a little message to tie the recipe in with the theme for the day and reinforce a biblical truth before making the recipe.

The appendices include a grocery shopping list; a supply list for the various arts, crafts, and activities; and a list of trinket and gift ideas for an optional countdown to Christmas.

I pray this book is a blessing to you and your family as you prepare your hearts for Christmas and enjoy the seasonal sights and sounds with your eyes firmly fixed on Jesus.

HOMESCHOOL *ADVENT*URE GUIDE

If you homeschool, you'll find many easy ways to incorporate this book into your daily routine. Whether you homeschool traditionally through the holidays or lighten the load to focus on more family fun, you can utilize this book as your homeschool *Adventure* guide! Each of the twenty-five chapters focuses on a specific holiday tradition, so here are a few ideas you can use to build upon the content of this book and implement the material into your lesson plans.

Bible Study & Scripture Memorization (Social Studies)

Each chapter begins with a Scripture, and additional Scriptures are included throughout each section. Depending on the ages of your children, you can focus on memorization, utilize the verses for copywork and hand-writing practice, or dive deeper into Bible study. You could also further explore the biblical lessons by searching out additional verses on the topic or use the verses for prayer journaling.

Language Arts & History (Social Studies)

Each chapter includes a family devotion that explores a common Christmas tradition, followed by a prayer and discussion questions. If you want to dive deeper into this section, you could study the history of each item with further research and notebooking. Depending on the ages of your children, they could write an essay or give an oral presentation on what they discover. They could also draw pictures or journal their favorite memories related to each tradition.

Math, Science, and More...

The final components of each chapter include a family adventure activity, a baking buddies conversation connection, and a recipe. The activity may be an adventure or simple craft to help you spend quality time together and reflect on the theme for the day. The conversation connection and recipe allow you to tie them together with the theme and reinforce a biblical truth. These make great homeschool activities as you can incorporate math, science, reading, and essential life skills into the quality time you spend together.

You can also ask additional questions as you work together in the kitchen, such as, "How many teaspoons equals one tablespoon?" or "What is one-half plus three-fourths?" You can talk about the science behind the baking process, like how baking soda acts as a leavening agent by releasing carbon dioxide gas to create the fluffy textures we enjoy in our baked goods.

Additional Resources

You'll find additional resources to help you as you homeschool through the holidays at KatieJTrent.com/Advent.

SECTION ONE

HOPE

1

HOPE IS A PERSON / ORNAMENTS

*So you see, just as death came into the world through a man,
now the resurrection from the dead has begun through another man.
Just as everyone dies because we all belong to Adam,
everyone who belongs to Christ will be given a new life.*
—1 Corinthians 15:21–22

What kind of ornaments do you put on your tree? Colorful balls? Handmade ornaments? Hundreds of colorful new options appear in stores each year. Do you enjoy looking at them? Our family does.

Have you ever wondered how the tradition of Christmas ornaments got started? Some say it began with the Adam and Eve feast day in Medieval Europe.[1] That was a big party held on December 24 in which people decorated trees with apples. Today, we see a wide variety of ornaments, but many are still shaped like balls—and look a bit like apples.

What do you know about Adam and Eve? Have you heard about how they disobeyed God after the snake tricked Eve? How they ate the fruit

---

1. "Adam and Eve Day," *Encyclopedia of Christmas and New Year's Celebrations*, 2nd ed. (2003), encyclopedia2.thefreedictionary.com/Adam+and+Eve+Day.

from the only tree God told them not to eat from? And how, because of their disobedience, sin entered our world?

You can read more about them in Genesis 1:26–3:7.

If the story stopped there, it would be rather sad. But thankfully, God sent Jesus to redeem us. Christmas reminds us of the hope for new life we find in Christ. It doesn't matter how badly we mess up; we can always turn to Jesus. *"O Lord, you are so good, so ready to forgive, so full of unfailing love for all who ask for your help"* (Psalm 86:5). Although the world around us may not exactly look the best, remember that our hope is found in Christ Jesus. And as we enjoy the ornaments on our Christmas tree, remember that hope is alive and lives in us when we ask Jesus into our hearts.

Prayer

God, thank You for rescuing us from our sins. Help us remember that no matter how bad or scary things may seem, we can always ask for Jesus's help. Amen.

Family Discussion Questions

» What mistake did Adam and Eve make?

» Have you ever made a really big mistake? How did you fix it?

» What does it mean to hope?

» Why do we put our hope in Jesus?

Family Adventure: HOPE Ornaments

Today we are going to make some ornaments to remind us that our hope can always be found in Jesus. (*The ornaments can be as simple or elaborate as you want. You can use construction paper, cardstock, or cardboard to cut out any shape and write the word HOPE in big box letters for your kids to color, or download my free templates at KatieJTrent.com/Advent.)*

Baking Buddies Conversation Connection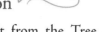

Adam and Eve sinned when they ate the fruit from the Tree of Knowledge of Good and Evil. Fruit is mentioned several times in the Bible. Have you ever heard of the fruit of the Spirit?

> *But the Holy Spirit produces this kind of fruit in our lives: love, joy, peace, patience, kindness, goodness, faithfulness, gentleness, and self-control. There is no law against these things.* (Galatians 5:22–23)

We are also taught that we should look at the fruit of other people's lives. *"Yes, just as you can identify a tree by its fruit, so you can identify people by their actions"* (Matthew 7:20). Today we are making What's the Fruit? Smoothies to remind us to pay attention to the fruit of our lives and the lives of those we choose to spend time with. Let's choose the fruit we want to use.

WHAT'S THE FRUIT? SMOOTHIE

Ingredients

3 cups frozen fruit *(or fruit mix)* of your choice
1¼ cup milk of choice *(regular, almond, oat, coconut)*
½ cup Greek yogurt or nut butter of choice *(for thickening)*

Additional items needed:

Blender or emulsion blender
Cups for sharing smoothie
Straws

Note: As you're preparing to put the fruit into the blender, you can talk about each type of fruit. Ask your children what they know about the fruit and like/dislike about it. Discuss how each of the fruits combine together to make different flavors and colors, and how people are different and unique too. You could also connect the discussion with the varieties of ornaments you see on trees for the holidays.

Directions

In a blender, combine all ingredients and blend until smooth. If the smoothie is too thick, you can add another tablespoon or two of milk and blend again until you reach the desired consistency.

Divide between 2-4 cups and enjoy.

1

LET JESUS LEAD / STARS

When they saw the star, they rejoiced with exceedingly great joy.
—Matthew 2:10 (NKJV)

During the holiday season, stars appear everywhere—from the tops of our Christmas trees to our cookie cutters. Can you see any stars in your house? How about outside your house? Why do you think stars are important?

In the story of Christmas, the star is significant because it guided the magi or wise men to Bethlehem when Jesus was born. It led them on a long journey to find Him.

Just like the bright, shining star that led the magi, Jesus promises to lead and guide us as we trust and follow Him. The Bible teaches us that God not only knows exactly how many stars are in the sky, but He actually gives them names. *"He counts the stars and calls them all by name"* (Psalm 147:4). Do you think you could count all the stars in the sky and remember all their names? I couldn't! Isn't God amazing?!

Did you know that you are far more precious to God than even the stars? He created only one of you in the whole wide world. God knows your name too, and if you will choose to follow Him all the days of your life, Jesus will never lead you the wrong way.

Whenever you feel sad, scared, or lost, just look to the sky and remember that the God who created the heavens and the earth created you too. He knows your name, and He loves you. He will lead you on the best path for your life. Proverbs 3:5–6 encourages us to *"Trust in the Lord with all your heart; do not depend on your own understanding. Seek his will in all you do, and he will show you which path to take."*

Prayer

Jesus, we trust in You and ask You to lead and guide us all the days of our lives, just like You led the magi. Amen.

Family Discussion Questions

> » Do you let the light of Jesus guide your life? In what ways?

> » Is it hard or easy to follow Jesus? Why?

> » How can you figure out what way Jesus wants you to go?

> » Since we can't follow a star in the sky like the magi, has God given us any other tools we can use to know His will for our lives?

Family Adventure: Following the Light of Jesus Flashlight Walk

Let's practice following the light of Jesus. We are going to play follow the leader. (*Either turn off all the lights inside or go outside at night. Have the leader shine a flashlight for everyone to follow.*) Notice how easy or hard it is to follow the light when you are close to it or far from it. Psalm 119:105 says,

"Your word is a lamp to guide my feet and a light for my path." (*Talk about how we want to stay close to Jesus by spending time with Him every day through prayer and reading the Bible. This makes it easier to follow Him.*)

Baking Buddies Conversation Connection

Ancient explorers used the stars to guide them to new lands, and we know that a star led the magi to Jesus. The North Star, also known as Polaris, is not very bright, but since it remains in almost exactly the same spot in the night sky, it provides a fixed point for determining which way is north. Jesus is like that. No matter how far we travel, He is always there, a beacon of hope in the darkest night. Psalm 25:4–5 says, *"Show me the right path, O Lord; point out the road for me to follow. Lead me by your truth and teach me, for you are the God who saves me. All day long I put my hope in you."* Today we're making Starry Grilled Cheese Sandwiches to remind us to always look to Jesus to guide us.

STARRY GRILLED CHEESE SANDWICHES

Note: Feel free to make your child's favorite sandwich, cold or hot, and then use a star-shaped cookie cutter to cut it into the shape of stars. If you don't have a cookie cutter, you can simply cut out a star shape with a knife (adults only).

Ingredients (family of 4):

8 pieces of your favorite bread (*I love potato or sourdough bread for these*)

4-8 slices of sharp cheddar cheese (*or your choice of cheese slices*) depending on how gooey you like your sandwiches

3-4 tbsp. butter or buttery spread

Additional items needed:

Electric griddle or frying pan and stovetop
Spatula
Cutting board
Star-shaped cookie cutter (*1" to 3"*)

Directions

Utilize an electric griddle or a frying pan and heat it to medium-low.

Butter one side of each slice of bread.

Once the pan is warm, place one slice of bread in the pan, butter side down. Add 1 or 2 slices of cheese on the bread, and then place the second slice of bread on top, with the butter side up. Repeat for as many sandwiches as fit on your griddle or pan.

Wait 1-3 minutes until bottom is golden brown, and the cheese has melted. Then, using a spatula, flip sandwich over and wait another 1-3 minutes until the other side is also golden brown.

Remove from heat to a cutting board. Carefully use the star-shaped cookie cutter or a knife (*adults only*) to cut the sandwiches into star shapes. *Warning, sandwich will be hot; use caution.*

Note: *Depending on the size of your cookie cutter, you can either cut out 1 star from the middle of the sandwich and serve both the star and sandwich with the middle star cutout, or you can cut multiple star shapes from the sandwich and just serve the stars.*

3

GOD CAN TURN IT ALL AROUND / DECEMBER 25

For a child is born to us, a son is given to us.
The government will rest on his shoulders. And he will be called:
Wonderful Counselor, Mighty God, Everlasting Father,
Prince of Peace. His government and its peace will never end.
He will rule with fairness and justice from the throne of his ancestor
David for all eternity. The passionate commitment of the LORD of
Heaven's Armies will make this happen!
—Isaiah 9:6–7

S-O-N, son, or S-U-N, sun? Do you know the difference? *S-U-N* means the star that shines outside during the day and is the center of our solar system. *S-O-N* refers to a male child. Jesus is described as the **Son of God** and the **Sun of Righteousness**. Both the sun and the Son are essential for life.

Do you know why we celebrate Jesus's birth on December 25 each year? It actually started with the sun. Long ago, this day was spent celebrating the change of seasons in what was known as *Sol Invictus* or the *Rebirth of the Unconquered Sun* after the winter solstice. There was a Roman festival called *Saturnalia* in which people had a big feast and exchanged gifts.[2]

But as God tends to do, He turned it all around. Did you know He often uses us, His sons and daughters, to turn things around here on earth? After the Roman Emperor Constantine gave his life to Jesus, he began changing things. By the year AD 336 (that's a loooonnnggg time ago), the Christian church in Rome started celebrating the Feast of the Nativity[3] on December 25, and this replaced Saturnalia.

Isn't it amazing how God turned that day around? Instead of worshiping idols, we now celebrate the birth of the unconquered Son of God! December 25 has become a day filled with light and love. It reminds us that there's always a reason to hope.

Imagine how people felt before Jesus was born. There was a lot of pain and sadness in the world. People had been waiting for a long time for a Savior, and most didn't even know that Jesus had been born until much later! But December 25 reminds us that God can *"make all things new"* (Revelation 21:5 NKJV). No matter how bad things may seem, there's always hope for tomorrow!

Prayer

Jesus, thank You for the hope You bring us. Help us to always remember that You promise to work everything out for our good. We need Your Holy Spirit to help us hold on to hope even when things are hard. Amen.

Family Discussion Questions

> » What does it mean to hope?

---

2. "Why Is Christmas in December?", *Encyclopaedia Britannica*, December 14, 2018, www.britannica.com/story/why-is-christmas-in-december.
3. "Today in History - December 25," *The Library of Congress*, www.loc.gov/item/today-in-history/december-25.

» Can you think of a story in the Bible in which God turned someone's life around or a bad situation into a good one? *(For example, the story of Joseph in Genesis 37–50.)*

» Can you think of a time in your life when something seemed bad but turned out good?

» How can we have hope when life feels hard?

Family Adventure: Mess into a Message Abstract Art Project

Adults: Scribble or put a line or an X on a page and have kids turn your mess into a masterpiece. See what sort of art they can create from a mess and remind them that Jesus turns our messes into messages of hope for others.

Baking Buddies Conversation Connection

Romans 8:28 says, *"And we know that God causes everything to work together for the good of those who love God and are called according to his purpose for them."* God promises to put the pieces of our pain and brokenness together to create something beautiful, like a puzzle. He works everything out for our good. Today we're making Picasso Puzzle Pancakes to remind us that sometimes the pieces don't all make sense by themselves, but together, they'll create a work of art, just like Pablo Picasso's paintings. *(Show your children a photo of one of his paintings, like "Three Musicians," or "Still Life.")*

PICASSO PUZZLE PANCAKES

(Thanks to Jennifer Dubose for sharing her dad's pancake recipe with us)

Ingredients

1 ¼ cup flour
2 ½ - 3 tsp. baking powder
2 tbsp. granulated sugar
¾ tsp. salt
1 large egg
1 ¼ cup milk
3 tbsp. oil
Butter or oil spray to grease griddle/frying pan

Topping ideas:

Maple syrup
Butter
Fresh fruit
Nut butter
Sprinkles
Whipped topping
Chocolate chips

Additional items needed:

Electric griddle *(or large frying pan and stovetop)*
Spatula

Knife or scissors for cutting shapes

Optional: Different shapes of cookie cutters, gel food coloring, or natural ingredients to dye the pancakes different colors (*matcha, freeze-dried raspberries, blueberries, turmeric, etc.*)

Directions

In a large bowl, whisk together dry ingredients (*flour, baking powder, salt, and sugar*).

Add in wet ingredients and whisk to combine.

Note: *Include a little extra milk or flour as needed to reach desired consistency. The batter should be thick, but able to flow easily off the whisk back into the batter.*

If you want the pancakes extra fluffy, add a pinch more baking powder.

For added fun, you can separate the batter into multiple bowls and add some food coloring or natural coloring agents (like beet powder, pureed or freeze-dried fruit, turmeric, matcha, etc.) to the batter to make different-colored pancakes for their artwork, though it isn't necessary since the toppings will add colorful fun too.

Heat an electric griddle or large frying pan to medium heat.

Lightly grease with butter or oil spray.

Pour batter onto heated surface in various shapes and sizes.

Once the batter bubbles all over (*1-3 minutes*), use a spatula to flip the pancakes over and cook on the other side. Repeat until the batter is gone or you have made enough pancakes for your family. (*You can cover and refrigerate the batter to use the next day if desired.*)

For the *Picasso Puzzle Pancakes*, cut the pancakes into various shapes (*cookie cutters work great, though a knife or kitchen shears work too*) and put them on a platter. Allow your kids to place the shapes on their plates to make unique designs before adding various toppings to create a masterpiece for their breakfast. (*Be sure to snap a photo of their artwork before they devour it.*)

4

SPREAD THE GOOD NEWS / CHRISTMAS CARDS

And then he told them,
"Go into all the world and preach the Good News to everyone."
—Mark 16:15

Jesus commanded us to go into all the world and spread His gospel to everyone. And while we may not be able to physically go everywhere in the world, there are many ways we can share the good news of Jesus with others. One of those ways is by sending Christmas cards to people near and far.

Have you ever sent or received a Christmas card? It's one of my favorite holiday traditions. Our family hangs them on the front door to enjoy throughout the season, and we love sending encouraging cards to family and friends too. What does your family do?

Did you know that people have been sending Christmas cards for nearly two hundred years? The very first Christmas card was sent by Henry Cole in England in 1843. He had 1,000 cards printed by his friend J. C.

Horsley.[4] It was a quick way for Henry to respond to all the people who were writing letters to him. Since then, the tradition has grown.

Christmas cards come in many shapes, sizes, and designs, but they all give you an opportunity to reach out and spread the hope of Jesus, tell people that you love them, and share some holiday cheer. This is a great way to minister to your family and friends.

You can also make cards for people you don't know. You could write to soldiers stationed around the world, bring cards to an assisted living facility, or even give to the homeless in your community. You can write encouraging messages and your favorite Scriptures on the cards too. You never know how a small act of kindness can leave a lasting impact and ignite hope. Don't forget to pray over the cards before you send them and pray for the people who send cards to you as well. They can serve as great reminders to pray for friends and family daily.

Prayer

God, please help me to spread the hope of Jesus in practical ways. Give me creative ideas for people to reach out to this Christmas season. Amen.

Family Discussion Questions

» How can a Christmas card spread the gospel of Jesus?

» Who would you like to send a card to?

» What are other ways we can tell people around the world about Jesus?

» What verses in the Bible fill you with the most hope?

---

4. John Hanc, "The History of the Christmas Card," *Smithsonian Magazine*, December 9, 2015, www.smithsonianmag.com/history/history-christmas-card-180957487.

Family Adventure:
Make & Send Christmas Cards

You can create your own with cardstock or simply fill out pre-made cards. Be sure to take a moment to pray for each person you're sending a card to.

Baking Buddies Conversation Connection

Jesus told His disciples, *"The harvest is great, but the workers are few. So pray to the Lord who is in charge of the harvest; ask him to send more workers into his fields"* (Matthew 9:37–38). Many people still need to hear the good news of the gospel, but too few are willing to share it with others. Today we're making Don't be a Grinch Christmas Punch to remind us not to be stingy in sharing the hope of Jesus with others. (**Note:** *If you want a healthier alternative, you could make Don't be a Grinch Salad, a green smoothie, cucumber bites, celery sticks, etc.*)

DON'T BE A GRINCH CHRISTMAS PUNCH

Ingredients

½ gallon lime sherbet

1 liter of lemon-lime soda

½ gallon Green Hawaiian fruit punch (**Note:** *If you don't like the kiwi-strawberry flavor of the punch, you could substitute lemon-lime Kool-Aid instead—1 pkg. lemon-lime Kool-Aid + 1 cup sugar + 2 qt. water.*)

Red sanding sugar for the rims of the glasses (*optional*)

Directions

Empty the sherbet into a large punch bowl.

Pour the soda and fruit punch (*or Kool-Aid made according to package instructions*) over the sherbet and stir to combine.

If you want to decorate the rims of the glasses, pour the sanding sugar onto a small bowl or rimmed plate (*large enough for you to dip the rim of your glasses into*).

Fill another bowl or rimmed plate with some shallow water.

Dip the rim of each glass in the water and then in the sanding sugar.

Ladle some punch into each glass and enjoy.

5

SEALED WITH GOD THROUGH JESUS / BOWS

Whatever is good and perfect is a gift coming down to us from God our Father, who created all the lights in the heavens. He never changes or casts a shifting shadow.

—James 1:17

Ever noticed all the big red bows at Christmastime? You'll find them as indoor or outdoor decorations and on presents. There's something so festive about a bright red bow. It's simple and yet it completes whatever it adorns.

Some people use bows as tree toppers, while others add them to wreaths or use them to seal gifts. You may also find them on streetlights, doors, mailboxes, and trees.

When I see those big, beautiful bows, I think of Jesus. Before Jesus began His ministry, He lived a simple life. His death on the cross and His resurrection are often referred to as His "finished work." Just like a bow finishes off whatever we place it on, so Jesus finished what He came to do. The red reminds us of the blood He shed for us so that we could live eternally with Him in heaven. And the bow reminds us that every good and perfect gift comes from God Himself.

So whenever you see a bright red bow this Advent season, remember that God sent His one and only begotten Son, Jesus, as the best gift we could ever receive. And when we receive Jesus as our Lord and Savior, we are forever sealed with God's promise of eternal life with Him. Those big red bows are a symbol of the hope we have through Jesus.

Prayer

God, thank You for sending Your Son Jesus as a gift for us so we can spend eternity with You. Help us remember His sacrifice this holiday season and share the gift of His love with others. Amen.

Family Discussion Questions

» What is the best gift you ever received? Why?

» What is something you want for your life that can't be purchased with money?

» Where could you put a red bow to remember what Jesus did for you?

» How does the life of Christ give us hope?

Family Adventure:
Make Decorative Crosses as Gifts

You can use cardstock to cut out the shape of a cross or cut long strips for the base and shorter strips for the cross and glue them together. Decorate the crosses with markers, stickers, jewels, etc. Once they're finished, punch a hole in the top and use a red ribbon to tie a bow to turn it into a hanging ornament or decoration. Finish the gifts by writing a little note with a promise verse and then give them to family, friends, neighbors, etc. Ideas for verses could include James 1:17 or John 3:16.

Note: *You could also make the crosses out of large popsicle sticks or purchase pre-made cross crafts (from wood or scratch art paper) for this activity.*

Baking Buddies Conversation Connection

The Bible teaches us, *"Now it is God who makes both us and you stand firm in Christ. He anointed us, set his seal of ownership on us, and put his Spirit in our hearts as a deposit, guaranteeing what is to come"* (2 Corinthians 1:21–22 NIV). Just as a bow seals a gift with the promise of something wonderful inside, so God has sealed us with His love—and He promises eternal life for all those who receive Jesus as their Lord and Savior. So today, we're making Sealed-With-A-Bow Puff Pastry Treats to remind us that we are sealed with Jesus forever.

SEALED-WITH-A-BOW PUFF PASTRY TREATS

Ingredients

1 package puff pastry dough *(thaw overnight in fridge)*
1 egg white
1 cup powdered sugar, sifted
½ lemon for zest and juice *(you can substitute 1-2 tsp. vanilla if you prefer)*
¼ cup chopped almonds (**Note:** *for nut alternatives, try pumpkin or sunflower seeds, or chopped pretzels*)

Directions

Thaw puff pastry dough overnight in the fridge.

Preheat oven to 375 degrees.

Prepare two baking sheets by lining them with parchment paper or using ovenproof silicone baking mats.

To make the glaze:

(Note: If you're making the vanilla glaze, simply combine 1 tsp. vanilla with the sifted powdered sugar and an egg white and then whisk together, adding more vanilla if needed to reach desired consistency.)

If you're making the lemon glaze, zest ½ a lemon into the bowl *(be sure you only zest the outside of the peel and not the white part, or it will be bitter; you can use a cheese grater if you don't have a zester).*

Sift powdered sugar through a sifter or fine sieve over the bowl to break up any clumps.

Whisk the zest and powdered sugar together.

In two small bowls, separate the egg white from the egg yolk. You can discard the yolk or use it in another recipe.

Pour the egg white into the bowl with the powdered sugar and zest.

In another small bowl, use a lemon juicer or squeeze the juice through your clean hand (*to prevent seeds from getting into the bowl*).

Add 1 tsp. of the lemon juice to the sugar mixture and whisk to combine. Gradually add a little more juice if needed to reach desired consistency. It should be smooth, but thick.

Unroll the puff pastry and use a pizza cutter (*or adults may use a sharp knife if preferred*) to cut the sheet. Start in the middle, cut the sheet in half, then cut each half into 8 even strips until you have a total of 16 strips (8 *from each half*).

Grab the top and bottom of a strip and twist your hands in opposite directions to create a bow (*the middle will have a couple twists and the ends will remain flat like a bow*).

Arrange the bows on your baking sheets, leaving at least 2" between them.

Brush the ends of the bows with the glaze and sprinkle with the chopped nuts, seeds, or pretzels.

Bake for 10-12 minutes, until the pastries are puffy and golden brown.

Remove from oven and carefully transfer to a wire rack to cool.

Note: *If you like your treat extra sweet, you can make a simple glaze with 1 cup powdered sugar, a splash of vanilla, and 1-3 tablespoons of milk (whisk to combine, adding more milk until you reach the desired consistency.) Drizzle over bows or dip them in the glaze and enjoy.*

6

GENEROSITY SPREADS HOPE /
ST. NICHOLAS

And don't forget to do good and to share with those in need.
These are the sacrifices that please God.
—Hebrews 13:16

During Christmastime, we celebrate the birth of Jesus. It's a time to remember that God gave us the greatest gift we could ever receive— His Son Jesus. Although nothing on earth compares to that gift, Christmastime is nonetheless marked by gift giving. Many people throughout history have generously spread Christmas cheer to others this way. Probably the most notable is Saint Nicholas. Do you know the story?

Nicholas was a bishop who was born around three hundred years after the death of Jesus. Legend says he heard of a poor man with three daughters who had no money to enable them to get married. So Nicholas secretly tossed gold into the girls' stockings, which were hanging by the fire. His gift gave hope to a family in the midst of a hopeless situation. Tales of his generosity continued to spread, and he eventually became Saint Nicholas—later known as Santa Claus.[5]

By the end of the eighteenth century, the legend of St. Nicholas spread to the United States. Today some families celebrate St. Nicholas Day on December 6 by filling stockings with little gifts, while others simply exchange gifts and stockings on Christmas Eve or Christmas Day. What does your family do?

Santa Claus is often associated with gifts at Christmastime, but the greatest example of generosity is found in the life of Jesus. He lived a life of service and sacrifice, giving hope and healing to a hurting world. The Bible teaches us in Proverbs 11:24–25 (NIV), *"One person gives freely, yet gains even more; another withholds unduly, but comes to poverty. A generous person will prosper; whoever refreshes others will be refreshed."* Whenever you see Santa Claus somewhere this holiday season, remind yourself to give generously to others just as God has given generously to us. You never know how a small act of kindness might spread hope to the hopeless as St. Nicholas's thoughtful gift did.

Prayer

God, thank You for giving us Your Son Jesus and for providing all we need. Help us to live unselfishly and spread the hope of Jesus wherever we go. Amen.

Family Discussion Questions

» How did St. Nicholas spread hope with his gift to the man and his three daughters?

» What do you think of when you see Santa Claus? Why?

» What does it mean to be generous? How can you be more generous?

---

5. Susan Hines-Brigger, "Saint Nicholas: The Original Santa Claus," *St. Anthony Messenger*, December 2022-January 2023, www.franciscanmedia.org/st-anthony-messenger/saint-nicholas-the-original-santa-claus.

» How does generosity spread hope and remind us of Jesus?

Family Adventure: Spread Christmas Hope

Spread some Christmas hope like Saint Nicholas today. Leave a surprise gift basket for someone (a neighbor, a nursing home resident, etc.), pay someone's bill at a restaurant or drive-through, shovel snow, donate clothes or toys, or find another way to give hope to someone this Advent. Talk about how it feels when we give generously to others instead of only thinking about what we are going to get.

Baking Buddies Conversation Connection

St. Nicholas and Santa Claus remind us of the power of generosity. In giving to others, they spread hope and Christmas cheer. As followers of Christ, we are called to love others and live a life of service and generosity too. The Bible teaches us:

Then the King will say to those on his right, "Come, you who are blessed by my Father, inherit the Kingdom prepared for you from the creation of the world. For I was hungry, and you fed me. I was thirsty, and you gave me a drink. I was a stranger, and you invited me into your home. I was naked, and you gave me clothing. I was sick, and you cared for me. I was in prison, and you visited me." Then these righteous ones will reply, "Lord, when did we ever see you hungry and feed you? Or thirsty and give you something to drink? Or a stranger and show you hospitality? Or naked and give you clothing? When did we ever see you sick or in prison and visit you?" And the King will say, "I tell you the truth, when you did it to one of the least of these my brothers and sisters, you were doing it to me!" (Matthew 25:34–40)

Today we're making Sweet Santa Hat Strawberries to remind us to sweetly spread Christmas cheer through generosity and service to others as Jesus has encouraged us to do.

SWEET SANTA HAT STRAWBERRIES

Ingredients

8 oz. cream cheese, softened
½ cup powdered sugar, sifted
½ tsp. pure vanilla extract
1 pint fresh strawberries
2-3 bananas *(cut into 20 pieces)*
20 lollipop sticks (**Note:** *You can use toothpicks, but with younger kids, you don't want a sharp point.*)

Directions

Rinse and pat strawberries dry with a paper towel.

Cut off the green leafy end of each strawberry so the bottom is flat *(to use for the Santa hats).*

In the bowl of your stand mixer with the paddle attachment *(or in a large bowl and using an electric hand mixer)*, combine cream cheese, powdered sugar, and vanilla. Mix until smooth and fluffy. Transfer to smaller bowls for dipping or place a dollop on individual plates for each child.

Peel the bananas. Cut off both ends and slice the remainder of the bananas into about 20 slices, approximately ¼ - ½ inch thick.

Place the center of a banana slice through the lollipop stick *(or toothpick)* and then place the strawberry on top of that *(inserting the wide flat side first so the small tip is at the top)*. You will have a banana slice brim under the strawberry hats.

Continue until all the strawberries and bananas have been made into Santa hats. Then, dip into the cream cheese mixture and enjoy.

SECTION TWO

PEACE/PREPARATION

7

LOOK TO JESUS / CHRISTMAS TREE

For my Father's will is that everyone who
looks to the Son and believes in him shall have eternal life,
and I will raise them up at the last day.
—John 6:40 (NIV)

Many homes have Christmas trees at the center of their festivities in December. Whether they are real or artificial, they all have the same basic triangular shape, with big branches at the bottom and shorter branches at the top. When I was a little girl, I loved to draw the angular lines of a Christmas tree. I would color garland zigzagging from top to bottom and add colorful balls to represent the ornaments.

In our home, we use an artificial Christmas tree because we love putting it up as early as we can. We like decorating the tree and enjoying its splendor for as long as possible. Do you have a Christmas tree? Is it real or artificial? When does your family put it up?

If you can, take a look at a Christmas tree. Do you notice how it's triangular in shape? This shape may help us think of the Trinity—Father, Son, and Holy Spirit—and draw our eyes toward heaven. Another thing you may notice about the Christmas tree is that most are either pine or fir trees. These are a special kind of tree known as evergreens, which means they stay green year-round. This reminds us that we have been promised eternal life through Jesus Christ.

Most people place a special decoration at the top of their tree, such as a star, a bow, or an angel. What does your family use? As we gaze up at whatever we place on the top branch, we can remember that everything in our lives, including our thoughts, should point us toward Jesus and the eternal life He bought for us through His death, burial, and resurrection. It also helps us to remember to point other people to Jesus too. Whenever you feel worried, scared, lonely, disappointed, or upset, remember to look up and focus on Jesus. And whenever you see a Christmas tree, say a little prayer of thanksgiving for our Savior.

Prayer

Dear heavenly Father, thank You for sending Your Son Jesus to die for us so that we can have eternal life through Him. Please work through us so our lives will point others to Jesus and help us look to You in every situation. Amen.

Family Discussion Questions

» What do you notice about your Christmas tree or a Christmas tree in your town?

» What do you worry about? What can you do when you feel upset, scared, or worried?

» What do you imagine heaven is like?

» What does it mean to have a new life in Christ?

» How can your life point others to Jesus?

Family Adventure: Pine Cone Bird Feeders

Have you ever noticed the ways God provides for wild birds? The Bible says, *"Look at the ravens. They don't plant or harvest or store food in barns, for God feeds them. And you are far more valuable to him than any birds!"* (Luke 12:24). God feeds our souls and takes care of our needs. Although God provides for birds, it is still fun to make them a special treat every now and then, so we're going to make some pine cone bird feeders.

Pine Cone Bird Feeder:

Items needed:

1 pine cone per person
1 jar of peanut butter *(for children with nut allergies, you can also use sunflower butter)*
Small bag of birdseed
Paper plates
String or twine *(cut into 12" pieces)*
Plastic butter knives or popsicle sticks

Directions

Scoop peanut butter onto one paper plate and dump birdseed on a second paper plate.
Loop the string or twine around the wider end of each pine cone. Tie a knot to secure it to the pine cone, and then use the ends to tie a loop for hanging.
Use a popsicle stick or plastic knife to spread peanut butter over the pine cone.
Sprinkle birdseed over the pine cone or roll the pine cone in the birdseed.
Tie the pine cone to a branch or another place in your yard for the birds to enjoy.

Baking Buddies Conversation Connection

Today we are making Better Than Birdfeed Trail Mix to help us remember that God is our provider and protector. First Peter 5:7 tells us, *"Give all your worries and cares to God, for he cares about you."* Whenever we are upset about anything, we can give those concerns to God because He cares for us even more than He cares for the birds.

BETTER THAN BIRDFEED TRAIL MIX

Ingredients

2 cups dry roasted peanuts, almonds, or nut mix of your choice
(*for nut allergies, utilize popcorn, cereal, or any other crunchy or salty
item you prefer*)
1 cup chocolate covered pretzels
1 cup mini holiday chocolate coated candies
½ cup semi-sweet chocolate chips
½ cup white chocolate chips
½ cup dried fruit of choice (*if desired to cut the sweetness*)

Directions

In large bowl, combine all ingredients.

Gently stir together.

Enjoy.

8

THE PEACE OF GOD / STOCKINGS

Search me, O God, and know my heart;
test me and know my anxious thoughts.
—Psalm 139:23

Does your family hang up stockings as part of your Christmas traditions? That custom began after people heard about the legend of Saint Nicholas in the fourth century in the country we now call Turkey. In other parts of the world, like Holland and Belgium, people put out shoes or boots for *Sinterklaas* to fill with small gifts and treats. These days, many families fill stockings with all kinds of goodies. What does your family do?

While most kids look forward to delicious treats and fun gifts in their stockings, some who've been naughty might find lumps of coal instead. How would you feel if you found coal in your stocking?

It doesn't matter how fun or fancy the stocking is on the outside, we all know it's what's inside that really counts. The same is true about us. It doesn't matter how nice we look on the outside; God teaches us to look at what's on the inside.

But the LORD said to Samuel, "Don't judge by his appearance or height, for I have rejected him. The LORD doesn't see things the way you see them. People judge by outward appearance, but the LORD looks at the heart." (1 Samuel 16:7)

What do you think Jesus would find if He looked inside your heart? Did you know that you get to choose what is in your heart and mind? Think about it. What are you listening to, watching, talking about, or reading? What thoughts do you let play over and over in your head? All of those fill us with either good or bad things, so we want to be sure to choose wisely.

Prayer

Jesus, search our hearts and show us anything that doesn't please You. Help us be mindful of what we fill ourselves with. Fill us with Your peace and let all that we think, say, and do be pleasing to You. Amen.

Family Discussion Questions

» What do you fill yourself with every day?

» How can you fill yourself with good things?

» What does it mean to *"guard your heart"* like Proverbs 4:23 suggests?

» Why do our thoughts matter? How can we change our thoughts?

Family Adventure: Make Your Own Stockings or Play the Fill-Your-Stocking Game

Make your own stockings or use premade ones to play the *Fill-Your-Stocking Game*. To play, find things that fit inside the stockings that best show who you are or what makes you special. It could be a toy car, a Lego character, a hair clip, stickers, jewelry, or anything else. Try setting a five-minute timer while everyone runs to collect items from around the house to place in their stockings. Gather back together after the timer goes off and share why you chose each item for your stocking.

For more fun, have someone else fill a stocking with what they think best represents you and talk about the difference between how you see yourself and how your family sees you. Then discuss how you think Jesus sees you.

Baking Buddies Conversation Connection

Our stockings can look nice on the outside, but we would like them to be filled with good things too. We have to guard what goes in us so that what comes out honors God. Proverbs 4:23 warns us, *"Guard your heart above all else, for it determines the course of your life."* That's why we're making Fill Your Heart with Good Fruit Pies today.

FILL YOUR HEART WITH GOOD FRUIT PIES

Ingredients

2 frozen pie crust rounds (*or you can make your own pie dough*)
12 tsp. jam or preserves (*use at least 2-3 types of jam so your kids can choose what to fill their hearts with*)
1 egg
1 tbsp. milk or milk alternative
¼ cup sanding sugar (*color of your choice or multiple options*)
¼ cup flour for rolling out the dough
Additional items you'll need:
Rolling pin
Parchment paper
1 large baking sheet
3" heart-shaped cookie cutter
Basting brush
Wooden skewer or fork (*to seal & decorate edges*)

Directions

Allow your pie crusts to thaw at room temperature (*follow the directions on the package*).

Line a large baking sheet with parchment paper. Set aside.

Lightly dust your counter, baking mat, or wax paper with flour and place pie crust in the center of the dusted surface.

Use a rolling pin to roll out the first pie crust so that it is a little thinner, and use your fingers to gently fix any cracks in the dough.

Use your heart-shaped cookie cutter to cut 12 heart-shaped pie crusts. Gently use a spatula to place each one on a parchment-lined baking sheet—at least one inch apart.

Allow each child to choose the type of jam they want to place in their heart pie. Scoop one teaspoon of jam into the center of each heart.

Lightly dust your surface with flour again and roll out the second pie dough the same way, then use your cookie cutter to cut out 12 additional heart shapes.

Place a heart on top of each of the pies. Use your fingers to gently press the edges around each pie to seal them. You can also use the flat end of a skewer to create decorative dots that help the seal or use the tongs of a fork to gently press all around the edges.

Put the baking sheet with the pies into the freezer to chill for 10-15 minutes to help them keep their shape as they bake.

Preheat the oven to 425 degrees.

In a small bowl, whisk together the egg and milk.

Remove the pies from the freezer and brush the tops with the egg wash, then sprinkle each one with sanding sugar.

Bake for 10-12 minutes, until the crust turns golden brown around the edges.

Allow pies to cool for 5-10 minutes before enjoying. *(Don't worry if some of the jam seeped out. It will still be delicious, and you can remind your kids that what's on the inside eventually comes out, which is why we want to be careful with what we put in.)*

9

LET YOUR LIGHT SHINE / HOLIDAY LIGHTS

*You are the light of the world—like a city on a hilltop that cannot
be hidden. No one lights a lamp and then puts it under a basket.
Instead, a lamp is placed on a stand, where it gives light to everyone
in the house. In the same way, let your good deeds shine out for all to
see, so that everyone will praise your heavenly Father.*
—Matthew 5:14–16

Are you curious about why people decorate their homes with strings of lights? The tradition began with a friend of the famous inventor Thomas Edison. Edison invented a string of lights in 1880 and hung them outside his laboratory that Christmas. Two years later, his friend, Edward H. Johnson, put a string of lights on his Christmas tree. Still, it took until 1903 for General Electric to start selling Christmas light kits, and another seventeen years before outdoor Christmas lights became popular.[6]

---

6. "Who Invented Electric Christmas Lights?", Science Reference Section, *Library of Congress*, November 19, 2019, www.loc.gov/everyday-mysteries/technology/item/who-invented-electric-christmas-lights.

Any adult will tell you that it takes a lot of work to put lights up outside the house, but people do it because it brings joy to so many. Have you ever looked at Christmas lights around your neighborhood? They make everything merry and bright while spreading Christmas cheer. Looking at Christmas light displays can make us feel both peaceful and happy, especially when the lights are dancing.

The Bible teaches us that we are called to light up this world and point people to Jesus. We can do that in many ways, like being kind and generous, helping those in need, sharing a smile, loving people who are mean to us, and being a friend to those who are lonely. How else can we let our good deeds shine out for all to see?

People are drawn to the light of Jesus that shines through us, so we want to look for ways to share His hope, peace, joy, and love with others.

Prayer

Heavenly Father, show me how to let the light of Jesus shine through me to bless those around me. Help me to light up the world with Your love this holiday season. Amen.

Family Discussion Questions

» How would you decorate your house if you could do anything you wished?

» Why is it important for us to shine our lights for others to see?

» How can we be the light of the world like Jesus?

» What is something you can do today to shine for Jesus?

Family Adventure:
Enjoy a Holiday Light Display

Go on a family walk or drive to enjoy the light displays around your community. For extra enjoyment, make hot cocoa, grab some snacks, and crank up the holiday music for your family adventure. Discuss what draws your attention and how the lights make you feel. Notice how the lights drive out the darkness and fill you with peace, hope, joy, and love.

Baking Buddies Conversation Connection

Just as Christmas lights brighten our neighborhoods at night, we can shine brightly for others when we love like Jesus. The Bible tells us that we are supposed to be salt and light for those around us. *"You are the salt of the earth. ... You are the light of the world—like a city on a hilltop that cannot be hidden"* (Matthew 5:13–14). We are told, *"Let your good deeds shine out for all to see, so that everyone will praise your heavenly Father"* (verse 16). Today we're making Salt & Light Salted Caramel Cookie Bars to remind us to be salt and light to those around us.

SALT & LIGHT SALTED CARAMEL COOKIE BARS

Ingredients

1 cup (*2 sticks*) unsalted butter, softened
1 cup light brown sugar, packed
½ cup granulated sugar
2 large eggs
1 tsp. vanilla extract
2 ½ cups all-purpose flour
1 tsp. kosher salt
1 tsp. baking soda
2 cups semi-sweet chocolate chips
14 oz. sweetened condensed milk
10 oz. soft caramels, unwrapped
1 tsp. flaked sea salt

Directions

Preheat oven to 350 degrees and line a 13x9" cake pan with foil, leaving a little to hang over two of the edges to easily remove the bars. Press the foil down around the edges.

Generously spray the foil with a nonstick cooking spray or rub with butter.

In a large bowl (*or the bowl of your stand mixer*), combine butter and both sugars. Mix with electric hand mixer or paddle attachment for your stand mixer on medium for approximately two minutes, until light and fluffy.

Add the eggs and vanilla and beat for another 1-2 minutes until combined.

In a small bowl, whisk together flour, kosher salt, and baking soda. Gradually add flour mixture into the mixing bowl and mix on low just until combined, scraping the sides of the bowl as needed.

Mix in chocolate chips with a spatula or wooden spoon.

Scoop half of the cookie dough into the bottom of the cake pan and press it down to make an even layer across the dish. (*It's okay if you use a little more than half. You want a solid layer.*)

Unwrap the caramels and have an adult place them in a medium-sized sauce pan on the stove.

Add in sweetened condensed milk and cook over medium-low heat, stirring constantly until the caramels melt. The mixture should be smooth.

An adult should carefully pour the caramel filling over the cookie dough in the cake pan.

Gently scoop out teaspoon-sized chunks of the remaining cookie dough and scatter them over the top of the caramel.

Bake for 27-33 minutes, just until the center is set and the cookie is golden brown.

Sprinkle the top with the sea salt flakes immediately.

Allow the bars to cool completely. Then, gently lift them out of the pan onto a cutting board using the edges of the foil. Remove the foil before slicing into bars.

10

GOD'S SWEET LOVE / CANDY CANES

How sweet your words taste to me; they are sweeter than honey.
—Psalm 119:103

While straight white candy sticks have been around since 1670, it wasn't until the turn of the twentieth century that iconic red and white striped candy canes were first made.[7] Those sweet treats have been enjoyed by children (and adults) for many years. Now candy canes come in a variety of flavors and colors, but there's something so Christmassy about the traditional red and white striped peppermint ones.

Did you know that these candy canes can remind us of Jesus? It's true! The shape looks like a shepherd's staff, and Jesus is known as the Good Shepherd, who sacrificed His life for us, His sheep. (See John 10:11.) And if you turn the candy cane upside down, it looks like a "J" for Jesus. Also, we may consider that the red represents Christ's blood that He shed for us on the cross, while the white reminds us that our sins have been forgiven and washed away. The two colors form stripes, and it is *"by His stripes we are healed"* (Isaiah 53:5 NKJV). And finally, the candy cane can remind us of

---

7. Lesley Kennedy, "Who Invented Candy Canes?," *History*, August 30, 2023, www.history.com/news/candy-canes-invented-germany.

the sweetness of God's love for us. (See John 3:16.) Who knew that such a little treat could have so much meaning?

Some people hang candy canes on their Christmas trees. Others place them in stockings. Still others give them as gifts or simply enjoy them as a sweet holiday treat. You'll also find tons of decorations shaped like candy canes—and even see images of them on wrapping paper. They are an iconic holiday tradition. Whatever you do with your candy canes, take a few minutes to thank Jesus for all He has done for you whenever you see one this holiday season.

Prayer

Jesus, thank You for Your great love for me. Help me to appreciate Your sacrifice each time I see a candy cane and let Your peace wash over me. Amen.

Family Discussion Questions

» What's your favorite flavor of candy cane?

» In what way do these sweet treats remind us of Jesus?

» How can words taste sweet like Psalm 119:103 tells us? And how can you use your words to spread joy and peace to others?

» How can you use a candy cane to share the gospel?

Family Adventure: Make Pipe Cleaner Candy Canes

Take one red pipe cleaner and one white pipe cleaner and line them up vertically side-by-side. Grab the top and bottom of both pipe cleaners and twist both hands in opposite directions so they look like stripes. Once the stripes are how you like them, curve one end to make the "J" shape. Hang your candy canes somewhere to help you remember Jesus this holiday season. (**Note:** *If you don't have pipe cleaners, you can draw a candy cane or use construction paper to make one.*)

Baking Buddies Conversation Connection

(**Note:** *The hot cocoa is rich and sweet, so if you'd like a lighter and healthier alternative, you can make Fun Fruit Canes instead.*) Today we're making Worth the Wait Slow-Cooker Peppermint Hot Cocoa to remind us of the importance of waiting patiently on God. The Israelites waited a very long time for Jesus to come—about four hundred years after the last Old Testament prophet, Malachi—and we are currently waiting for Jesus's triumphant return. Did you know that there are a lot of Bible verses about waiting on the Lord? Isaiah 40:31 (NKJV) says, *"But those who wait on the LORD shall renew their strength; they shall mount up with wings like eagles, they shall run and not be weary, they shall walk and not faint."* Sometimes we have to wait a long time to see our prayers answered, but just as the slow cooker is working while we wait, we can be at peace by trusting that God is working on our behalf too. That is always worth the wait!

Note: *If you're making Fun Fruit Canes instead, you can assemble the canes and then tell the kids they have to wait to eat them. Explain that when we pray to God, we want to trust Him to answer our prayers and keep our eyes focused on Him instead of what we're waiting for.*

WORTH THE WAIT SLOW-COOKER PEPPERMINT HOT COCOA

Ingredients

2 cups heavy cream
5 ½ cups whole milk
14 oz. sweetened condensed milk
1 tsp. peppermint extract
3 cups milk chocolate chips *(high quality)*
Topping ideas:
Mini marshmallows
Mini candy canes
Whipped cream

Directions

Combine cream, milk, condensed milk, peppermint extract, and milk chocolate chips in a slow cooker.

Set slow cooker to low heat and allow to cook for two hours, whisking occasionally.

Once the chocolate has melted completely and the mixture is hot, your cocoa is ready!

Serve in individual mugs and top with garnishes of choice *(whipped cream, mini marshmallows, and/or mini candy canes)*.

FUN FRUIT CANES

Ingredients (*per person*)

3 strawberries
1 banana
2 tbsp. nut butter, hazelnut spread, or yogurt

Directions

Cut the banana into slices at an angle (*so it curves when reassembled*) about ½ inch thick.

Wash and pat the strawberries dry. Then, cut off the green and discard it and continue slicing the strawberries in the same direction to make layers for the fruit cane approximately ½ inch thick. The tip will help with the curve of the cane.

Assemble the fruit on a plate by alternating a layer of banana, a thin layer of your spread of choice, and the strawberry. Repeat layers until your cane has been shaped, curving the top.

Be sure to instruct your kids to wait to eat the canes after they've been assembled and remind them that as we wait on God, we want to keep our focus on Him, not on our prayer or problem.

11

WORDS ARE POWERFUL /
CHRISTMAS GREETINGS

*Then the angel said to them, "Do not be afraid, for behold, I bring
you good tidings of great joy which will be to all people."*
—Luke 2:10 (NKJV)

You've likely heard someone say, "Merry Christmas" or "Happy holidays" this time of year. It's a common greeting. But do you know why we use these phrases? We see in the story of Jesus's birth that when the angel appeared to Mary, he brought *"good tidings of great joy"* or good news. As Christians, we want to greet people with good news as well.

The Bible refers to many different greetings. In 1 Peter 5:14, the apostle Peter tells us, *"Greet each other with a kiss of love. Peace be with all of you who are in Christ."* Another apostle, Paul, started all of his letters with greetings of grace and peace. These are blessings he proclaimed to Jesus's followers. Today, when we see someone, we greet them too. How do you greet people?

The word *Christmas* dates all the way back to AD 1038 and means the "Mass of Christ," or a gathering that celebrated the birth of Jesus. In medieval times, people wished each other happy *haliday* or "holy day." Eventually, this became "happy *holidays*" and included not only Christmas but also New Year's and feast days such as Epiphany, commemorating the wise men's visit to see baby Jesus, and Candlemas, which recalls Jesus's presentation at the temple in Jerusalem.

Whenever you hear or share holiday greetings this year, remember that we are celebrating holy days and the birth of our Lord and Savior, Jesus Christ. Be sure to give thanks to God for sending His Son so that we could spend eternity with Him.

Prayer

God, help me to always be thankful for Jesus and to celebrate this season in a way that brings honor and glory to Your holy name. Amen.

Family Discussion Questions

» Do you hear people say, "Happy holidays" more often than "Merry Christmas"? Why do you think that is?

» What are some occasions when you could wish someone "Merry Christmas"?

» How do you greet people other times of the year?

» What blessings could you release over people when you see them?

Family Adventure:
Write a Christmas Blessing

Our words can be powerful when we use them to impart blessings to others. We see this in Numbers 6:24–26 when the Lord told Moses to have Aaron and his sons bless the people of Israel with these words:

May the LORD bless you and protect you. May the LORD smile on you and be gracious to you. May the LORD show you his favor and give you his peace.

For today's family adventure, write your own Christmas blessing for your family, friends, or neighbors. Romans 12:14 tells us, *"Bless those who persecute you. Don't curse them; pray that God will bless them."* Think about promises from the Bible, what you wish for those you love—and even those who've hurt you—and which blessings you pray God will give to them. For example, your blessing might say, "Merry Christmas! May the Lord be rich in mercy and grace over your life. May the joy of the Lord be your strength forevermore and may His peace fill your hearts and minds continually. May He prosper you and fill you with hope. Amen."

Baking Buddies Conversation Connection

The Bible refers to Jesus as the *Word* in John 1:14: *"So the Word became human and made his home among us. He was full of unfailing love and faithfulness. And we have seen his glory, the glory of the Father's one and only Son."* The Bible also teaches us about the importance of our words. (See Proverbs 18:21.) Today we're making Merry Christmas Cookies—choose either gingerbread or sugar cookies—to remind us of the power of our words, and most importantly, the power of *the* Word, Jesus Christ.

MERRY CHRISTMAS GINGERBREAD COOKIES

Ingredients

¾ cup *(1 ½ sticks)* unsalted butter, softened
¾ cup dark brown sugar, packed
⅔ cup molasses
1 large egg
1 tsp. pure vanilla extract
3 ¼ cup all-purpose flour *(plus additional flour to roll out the dough)*
1 tbsp. ground ginger
1 tsp. baking soda
1 tsp. ground cinnamon
½ tsp. ground cloves
¼ tsp. ground nutmeg
½ tsp. kosher salt
Sugar cookie icing to decorate

Additional items needed:

Kitchen stand mixer or electric hand mixer
Cookie cutter letters to spell *"Merry Christmas"* and any other holiday shapes you want to use
Gel food coloring to dye icing if desired
Parchment paper or silicone baking mats
Rolling pin

Directions

In the bowl of your stand mixer *(or large bowl using an electric hand mixer)*, use the paddle attachment to beat butter, brown sugar, and molasses at medium speed until fluffy *(approximately 2 minutes)*.

Add in the egg and vanilla, and mix until incorporated.

In a medium bowl, whisk together flour, spices, baking soda, and salt to combine.

Gradually add dry ingredients to the bowl of your stand mixer, mixing on low just until the dough comes together. (**Don't overmix**)

Divide dough in half and create two round discs. Wrap each disc in plastic wrap and chill in refrigerator for 2-3 hours.

After dough has chilled, preheat oven to 350 degrees and line two large baking sheets with parchment paper.

Lightly flour your counter or other surface to roll out the dough. Take one disc out of the refrigerator at a time. Place disc on floured surface and use the rolling pin to roll the dough out until it's ¼" thick.

Use the cookie cutters to cut out the words "Merry Christmas" and any other shapes you want. Transfer the letters and shapes to baking trays, leaving an inch between each cookie.

Bake for 9-10 minutes until cookies slightly puff up. Allow to cool on baking sheets for 5 minutes before transferring to a wire rack to finish cooling.

With the scraps of dough from the first disc, press the dough back together into another disc, cover and refrigerate again while you work on the second disc of dough. Then, re-roll the dough and cut additional shapes. Continue the process until you've used all the dough.

Once the cookies have cooled completely, you can frost and decorate them.

MERRY CHRISTMAS SUGAR COOKIES

Ingredients

1 cup (*2 sticks*) unsalted butter, softened
1 cup granulated sugar
1 large egg
1 tbsp. milk
3 cups all-purpose flour
¾ tsp. baking powder
¼ tsp. salt
Powdered sugar for rolling out the dough (*approximately ¼ - ½ cup*)
Sugar cookie icing to decorate

Additional items needed:

Kitchen stand mixer or electric hand mixer
Cookie cutter letters to spell "*Merry Christmas*" and any other holiday shapes you want to use
Gel food coloring to dye icing if desired
Parchment paper or silicone baking mats
Rolling pin
Sifter or sieve

Directions

In a large bowl, sift together flour, baking powder, and salt. Set it aside.

In the bowl of a stand mixer or in a large mixing bowl (*with electric hand mixer*), beat butter and granulated sugar until light and fluffy using the paddle attachment.

Add egg and milk, then beat to combine.

Gradually add flour mixture and mix on low speed to combine. The dough should begin to pull away from the side. (***Don't overmix***)

Divide the dough in half. Place each half on a sheet of wax paper. Gently press dough into flat disks and wrap them in the wax paper.

Refrigerate dough for at least two hours.

After dough has chilled, preheat oven to 375 degrees.

Line cookie sheet with parchment paper and stick it in the freezer before you roll out dough. The chilled metal will help the dough keep its shape better in the oven.

Lightly dust your counter with powdered sugar.

Remove one disc of dough and unwrap it. Place it on powdered surface.

Sprinkle rolling pin with powdered sugar as well and roll out dough to approximately ¼" thick. Make sure you are moving the dough to assure it isn't sticking, and sprinkle a little more powdered sugar if needed. Note: *Move quickly to make sure dough remains chilled.*

Use cookie cutters to cut your shapes spelling "Merry Christmas" and whatever additional shapes you'd like to use.

Place cookies at least one inch apart on the lined and chilled baking sheet.

Bake for 7-9 minutes, until cookies begin to turn a golden brown on the bottom edges.

Allow to cool for 3-4 minutes on sheet before removing to a wire rack to cool completely.

Once the cookies have cooled completely, you can frost and decorate them using canned frosting and sprinkles, or by making a buttercream frosting or royal icing.

EASY ROYAL ICING RECIPE

Ingredients

4 cups powdered sugar
3 tbsp. meringue powder (**Note:** *Don't use plain egg white powder; it must be meringue powder*)
9 tbsp. water (*room temperature*)
*Gel food coloring as desired

Directions

In a large bowl or the bowl of a stand mixer, sift powdered sugar.

Add meringue powder and water to bowl of sifted powdered sugar.

Use the whisk attachment for your stand mixer (*or electric hand mixer*) and whip on high speed for 1-2 minutes.

When your icing is ready, it should fall from the whisk and smooth into the mixture within 5-8 seconds. It will get thicker the longer you beat it. If the icing is too thick, you can add another tablespoon of water and mix it together.

If you are coloring your icing, you can place it in separate bowls to add the gel color to and stir it in.

Note: *Royal icing takes longer to dry than regular frosting.*

12

OUR PRINCE OF PEACE / POINSETTIA

*Now may the Lord of peace himself give you his peace at
all times and in every situation.*
—2 Thessalonians 3:16

Have you ever seen a poinsettia? It's that beautiful red, leafy plant found everywhere at Christmastime. It's a common but unusual Christmas decoration considering it's a tropical plant from Mexico.

A Mexican legend tells the story of a young girl who had no gift for baby Jesus on Christmas Eve, but an angel told her to gather some weeds and bring them into her church. The weeds blossomed into the beautiful red poinsettia plant. In Mexico, they're known as *Flores de Noche Buena*, which is Spanish for *Flowers of the Holy Night*.[8]

The poinsettia was brought to America in 1828 by the first US minister to Mexico, Joel Roberts Poinsett, and the plant is named after him. Mr. Poinsett grew cuttings of the plant in his greenhouses in South Carolina, and it became very popular in the twentieth century. In fact, we now

---

8. "The Legend of the Poinsettia," *Farmers' Almanac*, December 1, 2023, www.farmersalmanac.com/poinsettia-legend-facts-trivia.

celebrate National Poinsettia Day on December 12, the anniversary of his death.

So what do poinsettias have to do with Jesus? The plants are commonly found in churches at Christmastime. To many people, the shape of the poinsettia resembles the star of Bethlehem that led the wise men to Jesus. Ancient Aztecs used the poinsettia to make dyes and medicines; they considered it to be a symbol of purity and peace. We know that Jesus is the *"Prince of Peace"* (Isaiah 9:6) and *"the sinless, spotless Lamb of God"* (1 Peter 1:19), so these beautiful Christmas plants can help us think of Jesus.

Prayer

Jesus, thank You for being our Prince of Peace. Fill us daily with Your peace that passes all understanding and guide us in our lives just as You guided the wise men to Bethlehem. Amen.

Family Discussion Questions

» What's your favorite color of poinsettia?

» How can poinsettias remind us of Jesus during the holidays?

» What does it mean to have peace?

» What do you need peace for right now?

Family Adventure: Make a Poinsettia or Purchase One

Make a poinsettia with paper or pipe cleaners, or purchase one from a store to remind you to turn to Jesus as your Prince of Peace. For craft templates, go to KatieJTrent.com/Advent.

Baking Buddies Conversation Connection

In John 14:27, Jesus tells us, *"I am leaving you with a gift—peace of mind and heart. And the peace I give is a gift the world cannot give. So don't be troubled or afraid."* Today we're making Red Raspberry Peaceful Poinsettia Fluff to remind us that the peace of God is a gift He gives us. We can rest in it, just as we will allow the fluff to rest and build a solid foundation before we finish and enjoy it.

RED RASPBERRY PEACEFUL POINSETTIA FLUFF

Ingredients

1 pkg. *(4.6 oz)* cook and serve vanilla pudding *(not instant)*
1 pkg. *(6 oz.)* raspberry jello mix
2 cups water
1 tsp. lemon juice
16 oz. whipped topping, thawed
2 cups raspberries *(if using frozen, thaw to room temperature)*

Directions

Caution, hot stove & liquid: In a medium saucepan, add pudding and jello mixes, water, and lemon juice. Bring to boil over medium heat, stirring constantly.

Once the mixture hits a rolling boil, remove from heat and carefully pour into a large bowl *(adults only)*. Cover the bowl with plastic wrap and refrigerate for 3 hours, or until the mixture has thickened.

Use an electric hand mixer to beat the mixture until it becomes light and fluffy.

Gently stir in thawed whipped topping to combine.

Add in raspberries and stir to incorporate.

Cover and refrigerate for another hour to chill before serving.

SECTION THREE

JOY

13

JESUS IS THE LIGHT / CHRISTMAS TREE LIGHTS

Look up into the heavens. Who created all the stars?
He brings them out like an army, one after another,
calling each by its name. Because of his great power and
incomparable strength, not a single one is missing.
—Isaiah 40:26

Would you like to know why we put lights on Christmas trees? According to legend, Martin Luther was captivated by the twinkling stars shining through the branches of some evergreens while he was walking home one night at Christmastime. He wanted to share this beautiful sight with his family, so he cut down a small tree, took it into his home, and placed candles on the branches.

Have you ever stared up into the night sky, tried to count the stars, and marveled at our incredible God? The Bible calls Jesus *"the light of the world"* (John 8:12) and teaches us, *"The heavens declare the glory of God"* (Psalm 19:1 NKJV). And what's even cooler is that this same God lovingly created each of us. He not only knows our names, but He knows the exact number of hairs on our heads. (See Matthew 10:30.) Even our parents don't know that!

So whenever you see lights on a Christmas tree, think about the stars and how awesome it is that God created you too! No matter how big a problem seems to be, God is even greater. And thanks to Jesus, we can go to God with all of our problems, and He will answer our prayers. (See John 14:13–14.)

Prayer

God, please help us to always trust in You, knowing how great and powerful You are and just how much You love and care for us. Amen.

Family Discussion Questions

- » Do you know how many stars are in the sky?

- » How is it possible for God to know the names of all the stars like it says in Isaiah 40:26?

- » What amazes you most in the world? How does that make you feel about God?

- » What do you need to trust God with today?

Family Adventure: Stargazing

Head outside tonight for some stargazing and enjoy the beauty of God's creation. *(Be sure to dress for the weather.)* Psalm 147:4–5 says, *"He counts the stars and calls them all by name. How great is our Lord! His power is absolute! His understanding is beyond comprehension!"* See how many stars you can name or have fun making up your own names for them. You can also play connect the star dots and see what kinds of pictures you could make in the sky.

Websites like in-the-sky.org will let you plug in your location and view an interactive map of the night sky that shows constellations, stars, and planets.

If it's too cold, too late, or cloudy, you can always turn the lights on your Christmas tree and enjoy the twinkling lights together instead.

Baking Buddies Conversation Connection

Jesus told people, *"I am the light of the world. If you follow me, you won't have to walk in darkness, because you will have the light that leads to life."* (John 8:12). Today we're making Light of the World Krispie Trees to remind us of Jesus, *"the light of the world."*

LIGHT OF THE WORLD KRISPIE TREES

Ingredients

9 cups crisped rice cereal
9 cups mini marshmallows
6 tbsp. butter
Green gel food coloring
White melting chocolate (*or a can of white frosting*)
Star-shaped sprinkles
Mini candies (*if desired*)

Directions

Spray two 8" round cake pans with non-stick cooking spray. Set aside.

Pour crisped rice cereal into a large bowl.

In a second, large microwave-safe bowl, add marshmallows and butter. Microwave 3-4 minutes, until marshmallows begin to melt together and puff up.

Carefully remove the bowl from the microwave. Add 3-4 drops of green food coloring and stir well.

Spray a spatula with the non-stick spray and pour marshmallow mix over top of the cereal. Use spatula to combine the cereal and marshmallow mix.

Divide mixture evenly between the two prepared round pans and use the spatula to press the mixture into the pans so that they are level.

Allow the treats to cool for approximately 30 minutes. Then, flip the pans over onto a cutting board to remove the treats from the pans.

Use a large, serrated knife to slice the treats like a pizza into six slices each to make your tree shapes.

Set up your decorating station with various sprinkles before melting the white chocolate (*it will harden quickly; use frosting if you want more time for decorating*).

Note: *If you want more precise decorating, you can use zipper sandwich bags as mini piping bags. Also, the white chocolate is very sweet, so you may choose to leave a few trees undecorated or limit the amount you use on the trees for decorating.*

Melt the white chocolate according to the package instructions. Place a few scoops into a plastic sandwich bag, pressing to remove the air and move the mix to the bottom corner of the bag. Twist the top to keep the icing from moving back up the bag as you squeeze. Use scissors to snip off a small piece of the corner to use it as a piping bag to decorate the trees.

Top with sprinkles and candies as desired.

14

MESSENGERS OF JOY / ANGELS

*That night there were shepherds staying in the fields nearby, guarding
their flocks of sheep. Suddenly, an angel of the Lord appeared among
them, and the radiance of the Lord's glory surrounded them.
They were terrified, but the angel reassured them. "Don't be afraid!"
he said. "I bring you good news that will bring great joy to all people.
The Savior—yes, the Messiah, the Lord—has been born today in
Bethlehem, the city of David! And you will recognize him
by this sign: You will find a baby wrapped snugly
in strips of cloth, lying in a manger."*
—Luke 2:8–12

Angels are found throughout the Christmas story—appearing to Mary,
Joseph, and the shepherds in Bethlehem. They were often known for
sharing joyous news with people. But did you ever notice how everyone was
afraid whenever angels appeared to them? In many stories throughout the
Bible, we are told that the people who saw angels were terrified, and the
angels always had to say something like, "Fear not!"

How do you think you would respond if you saw an angel? What do
you imagine they look like?

Angels are an important part of the Christmas story, and we often see them represented in decorations during Advent. Some people place angels at the top of their Christmas trees, while others decorate their homes with them. Many people enjoy collecting angel figurines. Do you have any angels displayed in your home?

Whenever you see an angel decoration, remember that they are known for spreading joy and being messengers for God. You can be a messenger for God too by sharing hope and joy with others. Look for opportunities to share the good news of the gospel with those around you.

Prayer

God, thank You for sending angels to guide and protect us. Help us to be sensitive to Your messengers and to share Your love with others. Amen.

Family Discussion Questions

» Why were angels important in the Christmas story?

» What do you know about angels? What does the Bible teach us about them? (*See Psalm 91:11; Matthew 18:10; Luke 2:8–12; John 20:11–13; Hebrews 1:7, 14; Hebrews 13:2.*)

» What role do angels have in our lives today?

» How can you make a difference in someone's life by being God's messenger of hope and joy?

Family Adventure:
Make an Angel Craft or Bless Someone

Make an angel craft or bless someone by being a messenger of hope and joy. (*Go to KatieJTrent.com/Advent for craft ideas and angel templates.*)

Baking Buddies Conversation Connection

Psalm 91:11 tells us that God *"will order his angels to protect you wherever you go."* Today we're making Angels French Toast to remind us that God's angels are on assignment to guard and protect us, and that we can be God's messengers too—sharing hope and joy with those around us.

ANGELS FRENCH TOAST

Ingredients

1 angel food cake *(store-bought and sliced into 12 pieces)*
3 large eggs
¾ cup milk
1 tbsp. flour
2 tsp. vanilla extract
¼ tsp. salt
¼ tsp. cinnamon
3-5 tbsp. butter or cooking spray to grease skillet or griddle

For the topping:

Maple syrup
Whipped cream
Fresh fruit *(strawberries, blueberries, etc.)*

Directions

In a measuring cup, whisk flour and a few tablespoons from the ¾ cup of milk together to create a slurry *(which helps the flour combine with the milk)*, then add the remainder of the milk.

In a large bowl, combine eggs, milk mixture, vanilla, salt, and cinnamon. Whisk together to combine.

Adults only: Heat a griddle or large skillet to medium heat. Use butter to grease it.

Carefully dip a slice of the angel food cake into the egg mixture (*with your hands or tongs if you prefer*), fully submerging the slice so it's coated on all sides. Pull it out of the mixture and allow the excess mixture to drip back into the bowl before placing it on the hot surface of your skillet or griddle to cook. Continue until you've got slices covering your cooking surface.

Allow each slice to cook for 20-30 seconds before flipping it over to cook on the other side. Once both front and back have cooked, use your tongs to place the thick back part on the skillet and cook for 20-30 seconds as well. Then, remove from heat, and continue the process until all the slices have been cooked.

Serve with the toppings of your choice and enjoy.

15

LET GOD'S LIGHT SHINE / CANDLES

For once you were full of darkness, but now you have light from the Lord. So live as people of light! For this light within you produces only what is good and right and true.
—Ephesians 5:8–9

The use of candles at Christmastime dates back to the Middle Ages when a big candle represented the Star of Bethlehem. Later, candles were used as lights on Christmas trees. Today, candles are often used in Advent wreaths.[9] Do you have any candles in your home? What do you use them for?

Candles at Christmastime remind us that Jesus is *"the light of the world"* (John 8:12). The Bible tells us, *"The light shines in the darkness, and the darkness has not overcome it"* (John 1:5 NIV). That means we have nothing to fear because Jesus has overcome the darkness. Isn't that wonderful?

No matter how bad things may seem, we already have victory through Jesus—and that's something worth celebrating! We see this truth in 1 Corinthians 15:57–58: *"But thank God! He gives us victory over sin and*

---

9. James Cooper, "Christmas Candles," www.whychristmas.com/customs/candles.

death through our Lord Jesus Christ. So, my dear brothers and sisters, be strong and immovable. Always work enthusiastically for the Lord, for you know that nothing you do for the Lord is ever useless."

It's comforting to know that when we accept Jesus into our hearts, His light shines through us too. We are meant to let the light of Jesus shine through us to bring hope and joy to others. So this holiday season, whenever you see a candle, let it remind you to shine the light of Jesus wherever you go.

Prayer

Jesus, thank You for overcoming darkness for us. Let Your light shine through us to bring joy to those around us every day. Amen.

Family Discussion Questions

- » Look at a candle. What do you notice about it?

- » What happens when you light a candle in a dark room? How is that like Jesus?

- » How can you shine the light of Jesus to those around you?

- » What happens when you move farther away from a lit candle when there are no other sources of light in the room? (*This is a good reminder to stay close to Jesus*).

Family Adventure: Sing Hymns or Carols by Candlelight

Light a candle and turn out all the lights. Sing your favorite hymns or Christmas carols. You could also give each person their own LED flameless candle to demonstrate how the joy of the Lord spreads from person to person. You can also find simple candle craft ideas at KatieJTrent.com/ Advent.

Baking Buddies Conversation Connection

What other special time of the year can you think of where we might use candles? *(Birthdays, for example.)* We're going to have an early birthday celebration for Jesus to remind us that we're celebrating His birth this Christmas. We're called to carry His light to others as He encourages us in Matthew 5:16 (NKJV): *"Let your light so shine before men, that they may see your good works and glorify your Father in heaven."* So today we're making *(choose your recipe)* Bananas-About-You Fruit Candles or Light-the-Way Confetti Cupcakes.

BANANAS-ABOUT-YOU FRUIT CANDLES

Ingredients

8 bananas

16 oz. of pre-cut cantaloupe chunks *(or you can cut your own 1"
chunks)*

8 strawberries

½ cup lemon juice *(juice from 1 lemon to keep bananas from turning
brown)*

16 mini chocolate chips *(or candy eyes)*

¼ cup cylinder-shaped sprinkles *(for mouth & wick)*

Also needed:

1" biscuit cutter or circle cookie cutter

Directions

Use the 1" biscuit or cookie cutter to cut 8 pieces of cantaloupe into
circles. Set aside.

Rinse the strawberries and cut the green stems off. Then, cut thin slices from top to bottom *(these will be the inner flames).*

Place a slice of strawberry on top of each circle of cantaloupe.

Cut the lemon in half and squeeze the juice into a medium-sized bowl.

Note: *If you don't have a lemon juicer, you'll want to clean your hands and hold half the lemon with the cut side facing down. Put the bowl beneath your hands and cup the other hand below the lemon. Squeeze the lemon so the seeds remain in your hand and only the juice filters through into the bowl.*

Peel the bananas and cut the ends so they stand straight like a candle. Gently toss them in the lemon juice to prevent them from browning. Then, lay them in a row on a plate or platter.

Place the cantaloupe circles with strawberry flames above each banana.

Put two mini chocolate chips *(or candy eyes)* on each banana about 1" from the top for eyes.

Add a sprinkle on top of the strawberry *(vertical line)* to look like a wick, and place a sprinkle in a horizontal line below the eyes for a mouth.

Encourage your kids to let their own lights shine for Jesus and enjoy your treats.

LIGHT-THE-WAY CONFETTI CUPCAKES

Ingredients

Cupcakes:
3 cups all-purpose flour
1 ½ tsp. baking powder
¾ tsp. salt
1 ¾ cup granulated sugar
4 eggs
¾ cup vegetable, avocado, or canola oil
1 cup milk
1 tbsp. pure vanilla extract
½ cup rainbow (*rod-like*) sprinkles + extra to sprinkle on top
Frosting:
½ cup (*1 stick*) unsalted butter, softened
8 oz. cream cheese, softened
2-3 cups powdered sugar, sifted
1 tbsp. milk
1 ½ tsp. lemon juice
½ tsp. lemon zest

Additional items needed:

24 regular-sized paper cupcake liners
2 muffin pans (*12 cups per pan*)

Stand mixer or electric hand mixer
Birthday candles
Sifter

Instructions

Preheat oven to 350 degrees. Place one paper cupcake liner in each of the 24 muffin pan cups.

In a large bowl *(or the bowl of your stand mixer)*, add flour, baking powder, salt, and sugar. Whisk together until combined.

Add in eggs, oil, milk, and vanilla. Then, use the paddle attachment or electric hand mixer to mix on medium speed for 2-3 minutes until smooth.

Pour sprinkles on top of the batter and use a spatula to gently fold them into the batter *(be careful as too much stirring will make the colors bleed)*.

Scoop the batter evenly in lined muffin cups *(I like to use a 1" cookie scoop)*. They should be about ¾ full.

Bake 15-20 minutes, or until the cupcakes have a slight golden-brown color and a toothpick inserted into the middle comes out with just a few crumbs.

Allow cupcakes to cool in the pans for about 5 minutes before transferring them to a wire rack to finish cooling.

Use another large bowl or the bowl of your stand mixer with the paddle attachment to make the frosting.

Add butter and cream cheese together and blend on high for 2-3 minutes with stand mixer or electric hand mixer until light and fluffy.

Sift powdered sugar over a separate large bowl to remove any chunks.

Add in the milk, lemon juice, lemon zest and about $^2/_3$ of the powdered sugar. Mix until smooth. You want the frosting to be thick, but spreadable.

If needed, gradually add in some of the remaining powdered sugar to thicken to desired consistency.

You can cover and refrigerate the frosting for 20-45 minutes if it seems too runny to pipe or spread on the cupcakes.

Use an offset spatula or piping bag to frost the cupcakes. Then, top with the remaining sprinkles. Place a candle in one of the cupcakes and sing "Happy Birthday" to Jesus before enjoying your treat.

16

GOD'S GIFTS IN US / WRAPPING GIFTS

And this will be the sign to you: You will find a Babe wrapped in swaddling cloths, lying in a manger.
—Luke 2:12 (NKJV)

Have you ever thought about why we wrap gifts instead of just giving them to people? The custom dates back to Victorian England in the 1800s, after the invention of the Christmas card. With advancements in the printing industry, Victorian Christmas paper was created to match the new Christmas cards being printed. Soon, decorated boxes and bags emerged as well.[10]

But long before we wrapped presents and exchanged them on Christmas, the very first and best Christmas gift was wrapped in strips of cloth. Do you know what that gift was? Jesus! He was born in a manger and wrapped in swaddling cloths in the town of Bethlehem, which fulfilled many Old Testament prophecies. Here are a few of them:

---

10. Gillian S. Holmes, "Wrapping Paper," *Encyclopedia.com*, May 29, 2018, www.encyclopedia.com/science-and-technology/technology/technology-terms-and-concepts/wrapping-paper.

Then the LORD said … "I will raise up a prophet like you from among their fellow Israelites. I will put my words in his mouth, and he will tell the people everything I command him." (Deuteronomy 18:17–18)

The Lord himself will give you the sign. Look! The virgin will conceive a child! She will give birth to a son and will call him Immanuel (which means "God is with us"). (Isaiah 7:14)

But you, O Bethlehem Ephrathah, are only a small village among all the people of Judah. Yet a ruler of Israel, whose origins are in the distant past, will come from you on my behalf. (Micah 5:2)

In fact, Jesus's life fulfilled over three hundred promises God gave about Jesus before He was sent to earth. That's pretty miraculous!

Wrapped gifts are like a promise of what's to come. They show that someone took extra care to prepare something special for us to unwrap. Did you know that God actually sent many wonderful promises for us to unwrap and discover too? The Bible is filled with them. And because God fulfilled so many prophesies when He sent Jesus, we can trust Him to fulfill all of His promises to us too.

The next time you give or receive a wrapped gift, remember that God has wrapped wonderful gifts inside of you and has lots of promises for you to discover as you read the Bible, pray, and spend time in His presence— which is better than any other present you could ever receive! And the greatest gift you could ever share with anyone else is the gift of eternal life found only through a relationship with Jesus Christ, our Lord and Savior.

Prayer

God, thank You for giving us the greatest gift of all. Help us to unwrap all of the promises found in Your Word and discover the gifts You've hidden within each of us. Amen.

Family Discussion Questions

» Why do you think people like to wrap gifts before giving them?

» Can you think of a promise God gave us in Scripture that you've discovered or "unwrapped" recently?

» What types of gifts does the Bible say God gives to us? (*See Romans 12:4–8; 1 Corinthians 12; Ephesians 4:5–16.*)

» What is one gift you have that you can share with others?

Family Adventure: Play the Plastic Wrap Gift Game or Wrap & Deliver a Gift

To play the game, gather small items, candies, coins, etc. for prizes. Wrap the first item in several layers of plastic wrap to make a ball shape. Add a second small prize on top and keep wrapping layers and adding more prizes until you have a large ball filled with numerous items. Take a set of dice and a pair of oven mitts and have everyone sit in a circle.

One person rolls the dice until they get doubles (two of the same number). As soon as they get doubles, they pass the dice to the person on their left, put on the oven mitts, and begin trying to unwrap the gift ball with the oven mitts on. They get to keep any prizes that fall out while it's their turn. Once the next person rolls doubles, the first person's turn ends, and they pass the ball and mitts to the second person. The dice go to the next person on the left, and play continues until all the prizes have been unwrapped.

Note: If you don't want to play the game, you could purchase or make a gift, wrap it, and deliver it to someone special.

Baking Buddies Conversation Connection

Jesus was the greatest gift we could ever receive, and He was wrapped in swaddling cloths at birth. And 1 Peter 4:10 tells us, *"God has given each of you a gift from his great variety of spiritual gifts. Use them well to serve one another."* Just as Jesus was wrapped as a gift for us, so God has wrapped gifts inside each of us, and He wants us to use those gifts to transform the world around us for His glory. We're making Wrapped Like Jesus wraps today to remind us of that special night long ago when God sent the greatest gift, His Son, to us. *(You choose wrap filling: peanut butter and jelly, turkey and cheese, or scrambled eggs and cheese.)*

WRAPPED LIKE JESUS (PB&JS, TURKEY CHEESE WRAPS, OR SCRAMBLED EGG WRAPS)

Ingredients

PB&J Wrap

    1 tortilla per person
    1 tbsp. peanut butter per person (or nut butter, hazelnut spread, alternative butter, etc.)
    1 tbsp. jam of choice per person

Directions

Lay tortilla flat on a cutting board.

Spread a layer of peanut butter *(or other nut spread)* around the tortilla, leaving a 1" border all the way around the outer edge with no spread.

Spread a thin layer of jam over the top of the nut butter, again leaving the outer edge without any spread.

Fold the left and right edges in 1," then roll from the bottom to the top to wrap the tortilla like a burrito.

Continue process with as many tortillas as you need to feed your family.

Enjoy.

Turkey Cheese Wraps

1 tortilla per person
2-3 slices of lunch meat per person
1-2 slices of cheese per person (*or handful of shredded cheese*)
1-2 tbsp. mayonnaise and/or mustard if desired

Directions

Lay tortilla flat on a cutting board.

Spread a layer of mayonnaise or mustard around the tortilla, leaving a 1" border all the way around the outer edge with no spread.

Place the lunch meat over the tortilla, leaving 1" border open around the edge.

Add cheese on top of the meat.

Fold the left and right edges in 1," then roll from the bottom to the top to wrap the tortilla like a burrito.

Continue process with as many tortillas as you need to feed your family.

Enjoy.

Scrambled Egg and Cheese Wraps

1 tortilla per person
2 eggs per person, scrambled
1 slice (*or a handful of shredded cheese*) per person

Directions

Note: An adult should make this recipe since it involves a hot stove, pan, and eggs.

Crack the eggs (*enough for each person*) into a bowl and whisk together.

Heat a skillet to medium heat and spray with nonstick cooking spray.

Pour in the eggs and allow them to cook for 1-2 minutes. Use a spatula to flip the eggs and chop them into smaller chunks. Continue until the eggs are fully cooked, then remove from heat.

Lay tortillas flat on a cutting board (*enough for each person*).

Spread a thin layer of scrambled eggs around the tortillas, leaving a 1" border all the way around the outer edge with no eggs.

Sprinkle eggs with cheese.

Carefully fold the left and right edges of the tortilla in 1," then roll from the bottom to the top to wrap it like a burrito.

Continue process with as many tortillas as you need to feed your family.

Enjoy.

17

GOD LOVES A CHEERFUL GIVER / HOLIDAY BAKING

Taste and see that the Lord is good.
Oh, the joys of those who take refuge in him!
—Psalm 34:8

The Advent season is filled with yummy treats, sights, and smells. Some of my favorite memories are of my mom baking holiday cookies. Our family has carried on the tradition of holiday baking, and we love to bless others with goodies at Christmastime. Do you have a favorite holiday treat?

A few years ago, after we moved into a new neighborhood, we baked a bunch of cookies and miniature cakes and went door to door to deliver them to our new neighbors. To this day, we hear stories from people who were incredibly blessed by that simple act of kindness. Many were far from family and feeling lonely during the holidays, so receiving a homemade treat deeply impacted them. We were able to spread joy and share the love of Jesus in a very tangible way. It has become one of our family's favorite holiday traditions!

Sharing food isn't a new idea. In fact, we see Jesus feeding people throughout the Bible. Not only is holiday baking fun and delicious, it's actually a great way to remember Jesus and share His love with others too. When you deliver homemade treats to people, you are being the hands and feet of Jesus. So, whenever you make or receive a baked good this year, remember how Jesus shared His love with everyone He encountered.

Prayer

Jesus, help us to share Your love wherever we go and to be sensitive to the needs of people around us. Amen.

Family Discussion Questions

» What is your favorite holiday treat to eat?

» What's your favorite holiday treat to bake? Why?

» How can baking spread the love and joy of Jesus?

» Who would you like to make a special treat for? Why?

Family Adventure: Bake & Deliver Holiday Treats

Bake and deliver holiday treats to people in your neighborhood, at church, or in your community to spread some holiday cheer. You can use today's recipe or make your own family favorite.

Baking Buddies Conversation Connection

Everyone loves homemade chocolate chip cookies, so today we're making Mom's Cheerful Chocolate Chip Cookies to help us spread Christmas cheer to others. Luke 6:35–36 (NIV) says, "*Love your enemies, do good to them, and lend to them without expecting to get anything back. Then your reward will be great, and you will be children of the Most High, because he is kind to the ungrateful and wicked. Be merciful, just as your Father is merciful."* Today we're putting both white chocolate and semi-sweet chocolate chips in the cookies to remind us to be the light in the darkness today and always.

MOM'S CHEERFUL CHOCOLATE CHIP COOKIES (DOUBLE BATCH FOR SHARING)

Ingredients

4 ½ cups all-purpose flour

2 tsp. baking soda

2 tsp. kosher salt

2 cups (2 *sticks*) butter-flavored shortening (*Note: You can use 4 sticks of butter instead, but the shortening makes the cookies come out with the perfect texture and flavor.*)

1 ½ cups granulated sugar

1 ½ cups brown sugar (*packed*)

2 tsp. pure vanilla extract

4 large eggs

2 cups (*12 oz. package*) semi-sweet chocolate chips

2 cups (*12 oz. package*) white chocolate chips

Note: *Divide all ingredients in half if you want to make a single batch instead*

Directions

Preheat oven to 375 degrees and line two baking sheets with parchment paper. Set aside. (*Note: Using multiple trays will make the process quicker so you can rotate batches easily.*)

In a large bowl, combine flour, baking soda, and salt. Whisk together.

In the bowl of your stand mixer *(or another large mixing bowl)*, use the paddle attachment *(or electric hand mixer)* to cream the butter-flavored shortening, both sugars, and vanilla together on medium speed.

Add the eggs in one at a time, beating well after each egg so the mixture is creamy.

Gradually add in the flour mixture just until combined.

Pour in both types of chocolate chips and use a sturdy spoon or spatula to mix them throughout the batter.

Use a small cookie scoop *(or drop by rounded tablespoon)* onto the lined baking sheets.

Bake one tray for 9-10 minutes until golden brown *(Don't overbake.)* Allow the cookies to cool for 2-3 minutes before transferring to a wire rack to cool completely. Continue process until all the dough has been baked.

Place cooled cookies in small treat bags or on decorative paper plates and deliver with a little note to spread Christmas cheer.

18

SPREAD THE GOSPEL / CAROLING

Let the message about Christ, in all its richness, fill your lives. Teach and counsel each other with all the wisdom he gives. Sing psalms and hymns and spiritual songs to God with thankful hearts.
—Colossians 3:16

Christmas season officially kicks off when we start hearing Christmas music everywhere—in stores, restaurants, and on the radio. Do you have a favorite Christmas carol? While there are many Christmas songs about a variety of topics, Christmas carols are specifically about the birth of our Lord and Savior, Jesus Christ.

How many Christmas carols can you think of? Some popular songs include "Joy to the World," "O Come All Ye Faithful," "O Holy Night," "The First Noel," "Silent Night," "Away in a Manger," "We Three Kings," "God Rest Ye Merry Gentlemen," and "Angels We Have Heard on High"—just to name a few. Each of these carols focus on that special night when Christ was born.

When we sing Christmas carols, we are proclaiming the good news of the gospel for all to hear. Who knew that singing carols could actually have an eternal impact on listeners? Not only is caroling a great evangelistic tool, it's also a wonderful way to spread Christmas cheer and make connections throughout our communities. We're able to interact with neighbors and bless groups of people at assisted living facilities, homeless shelters, orphanages, hospitals, or other places where people are lonely, hurt, or suffering. We get to be the hands and feet of Jesus in a fun and meaningful way whenever we go caroling.

God delights in our singing too! Psalm 147:1 tells us, *"Praise the Lord! How good to sing praises to our God! How delightful and how fitting!"* You'll find many more verses about singing to God throughout the Bible. When you hear a Christmas carol, take a moment to praise God and express thanksgiving to Him because He is so worthy of our praise!

Prayer

God, we praise Your holy name. Thank You for the joy of music and songs. Help us to sing Your praises daily. Amen.

Family Discussion Questions

> » What is your favorite Christmas carol and why?

> » Why do you think songs have such a big impact on our lives?

> » What does it mean to praise God?

> » How can Christmas carols spread the gospel of Jesus?

Family Adventure: Go Caroling

Sing your favorite Christmas carols together. You can sing at home or spread Christmas cheer by singing carols around your neighborhood, at church, or in your community (*hospital, senior center, homeless shelter, etc.*).

Baking Buddies Conversation Connection

King David was having a hard time in his life when he wrote this psalm:

But as for me, I will sing about your power. Each morning I will sing with joy about your unfailing love. For you have been my refuge, a place of safety when I am in distress. O my Strength, to you I sing praises, for you, O God, are my refuge, the God who shows me unfailing love.

(Psalm 59:16–17)

Whether things are going well or we're in the middle of a struggle, these verses remind us that God is always faithful. He is a bright light, even on a dark day—and singing praise to Him releases joy to us and to others. Today we're making Cranberry Christmas Carol Cake to remind us to be a bright spot in people's lives by spreading Christmas cheer wherever we go.

CRANBERRY CHRISTMAS CAROL CAKE

Ingredients

3 eggs
2 cups granulated sugar
¾ cup unsalted butter, softened (*1 ½ sticks*)
1 tsp. pure vanilla extract
2 cups all-purpose flour
12 oz. fresh or frozen cranberries

Directions

Preheat oven to 350 degrees.

Grease a 13x9" cake pan with cooking spray or butter. Set aside.

In the bowl of your stand mixer (*or large mixing bowl*), combine eggs and sugar. Use paddle attachment (*or electric hand mixer*) to mix on medium speed until light and fluffy (*2-3 minutes*).

Add butter and vanilla and mix for another two minutes.

Mix in flour just until combined.

Pour in cranberries and mix with a spoon or spatula so they spread throughout the batter.

Use a spatula or offset spatula to spread the batter into the pan in an even layer (*it will be thick*).

Bake 40-50 minutes until the cake is golden brown and a toothpick inserted in the center comes out clean.

Allow cake to cool before slicing.

SECTION FOUR

LOVE

19

LOVE LIKE JESUS / WREATH

Live a life filled with love, following the example of Christ. He loved
us and offered himself as a sacrifice for us, a pleasing aroma to God.
—Ephesians 5:2

We see a lot of wreaths at Christmastime. People put them on their doors and decorate their homes with them. Do you have a wreath anywhere in or on your home? Did you know that people originally hung wreaths on their Christmas trees? The tradition started in the sixteenth century when Europeans trimmed branches on Christmas trees and then used the excess branches to create wreaths.[11]

Did you know that wreaths represent love? The circular shape is a symbol of God's unending love, which has no beginning and no end. The circle reminds us of what the Bible teaches us about God:

"I am the Alpha and the Omega—the beginning and the end," says the
Lord God. "I am the one who is, who always was, and who is still to
come—the Almighty One." (Revelation 1:8)

11. Kat Moon, "Christmas Wreaths Are a Classic Holiday Decoration With a Surprisingly Deep History," *Time Magazine*, December 21, 2018, time.com/5482144/christmas-wreath-origins.

Wreaths tend to be made from evergreen trees, which represent eternal life and resilience in the face of difficulties. They also remind us of Jesus's sacrificial love for us. Can you think of anything else used to symbolize eternal love?

Did you know that wedding rings represent unending love? Additionally, they are an outward expression of someone's commitment to their spouse. The next time you see a wreath, let it remind you of Christ's unending love and commitment to you.

Prayer

God, thank You for Your faithfulness and unending love for us. Thank You for sending Jesus so we can live eternally with You. Help us always remember Your perfect love for us. Amen.

Family Discussion Questions

» How do wreaths remind us of God?

» How do you know Jesus loves you?

» What does unconditional love mean?

» How can you share the love of Jesus with others?

Family Adventure: Make Handprint Wreaths or Give Promise Rings

Many people give their kids promise rings as a symbol of purity or devotion to Jesus. You could gift your children with rings to remind them of their commitment to Jesus or create your own wreaths to decorate your house today. For the wreath, you can trace your kids' hands on green construction paper, cut them out, and then glue them in a circle to make the wreath shape. Add a bow, red holly berries, or other decorations. You could also write promise verses on each hand to remember God's love for us. (*For example, Psalm 36:5, 7; Lamentations 3:22; John 3:16; John 15:9; Romans 5:8; Romans 8:35–39; Ephesians 2:4–5; 1 John 4:7–12.*)

Baking Buddies Conversation Connection

Colossians 3:14 says, "*Above all, clothe yourselves with love, which binds us all together in perfect harmony.*" Today we're making Wrapped in God's Love Hotdog Wreaths *or* Sealed with God Marshmallow Wreaths (*your choice*) to remind us of God's unending love for us.

WRAPPED IN GOD'S LOVE HOTDOG WREATHS

Ingredients

1 tube refrigerated crescent roll dough
24 miniature hotdogs
¼ cup Dijon mustard
1 egg and splash of milk *(to make an egg wash)*
Sprinkle of kosher salt
Rosemary sprigs for decoration *(optional)*
Ketchup and/or Dijon mustard for dipping

Directions

Preheat oven to 375 degrees and line a large baking sheet with parchment paper. Set aside.

Slice each triangle crescent roll into thirds lengthwise *(to make 3 thinner triangular-shaped slices)*.

Brush the tops of the rolls with Dijon mustard.

Place one mini hotdog at the thick end of the triangle and roll the hotdog up in the crescent dough. Continue until all 24 hotdogs are wrapped in crescent rolls.

Arrange the rolls side by side *(with dough touching)* in a circle on the baking sheet so that they will connect as they bake. (**Note:** *You can also arrange them into a smaller, thicker wreath by arranging about 9-10 of them into the inner wreath and the remainder into the outer wreath.)*

In a small bowl, mix egg and splash of milk with a fork, then brush the egg wash over all of the rolls.

Lightly sprinkle the top of the wreath with salt.

Bake 15-20 minutes, until the rolls are golden brown.

Allow to cool for 20 minutes and place rosemary around the inside of the wreath before serving, if desired. Enjoy plain or dip in mustard or ketchup.

SEALED WITH GOD MARSHMALLOW WREATHS

Ingredients

4 cups mini marshmallows
½ cup salted butter
1 tsp. green gel food coloring
½ tsp. pure vanilla extract
½ tsp. almond extract
4 cups cornflake cereal
2 ¼ oz. cinnamon red hot candies

Additional items needed:

1"-2" round biscuit or cookie cutter
Non-stick cooking spray

Directions

Line a large baking sheet with parchment paper and set aside.

Place marshmallows and butter in a large, microwave-safe bowl. Microwave on high for two minutes. Carefully remove bowl from microwave and stir, then return bowl to microwave for another two minutes, or until the mixture is completely melted.

Add the food coloring, vanilla, and almond extract into the mixture and stir to combine.

Pour cornflakes into the bowl and gently fold them in to evenly coat the cereal with the marshmallow mixture.

Lightly grease a 1"-2" circle biscuit or cookie cutter and your hands.

Scoop out a handful (*or about half a cup*) of the mixture and gently shape it around the cutter to form a circle. Lightly press the mixture together, but be careful not to crush the cereal.

Lift out the cutter and then place three pieces of candy together in a triangle on one part of the wreath for decoration. Continue until you've made all the wreaths.

Allow wreaths to cool and then enjoy.

20

THE GREATEST GIFT /
OPENING PRESENTS

For God so loved the world that He gave His only begotten Son, that whoever believes in Him should not perish but have everlasting life.
—John 3:16 (NKJV)

I'll never forget the year I got a tree stand for Christmas. Yes, you read that right: the thing that holds up a Christmas tree. I was a young girl eager to open a gift from my grandma, but my excitement turned to confusion when I unwrapped the present to find a tree stand box instead of a toy.

My mother always taught me to be grateful, so I pushed down my disappointment and forced myself to smile and thank my grandma for the gift. Of course, she laughed and told me to open the box and look inside. I couldn't tell you what the gift was, but I know it was much better than the tree stand! I felt so relieved—and a little silly—for thinking she would give me such a terrible present. But that lesson is one that has stuck with me all these years.

Just imagine if I had never opened the box. It could have held the greatest gift of all time, but unless I opened the gift—and used it—it wouldn't do me any good.

The same is true of Jesus. He *was* and *is* the greatest gift that has ever been given, but it's up to us to accept or reject His gift. Once we accept Jesus as our Lord and Savior, we need to utilize His gift and not just stick it on a shelf to collect dust—because Jesus didn't die just for us to go to heaven one day. He died so we could bring heaven to earth through a personal relationship with Him in order for many more people to hear about and receive His gift of eternal life.

So, whenever you see a present, let it remind you that we have *already received the greatest gift of all*—the gift of salvation paid for by our loving Savior, Jesus Christ. That is the reason we celebrate Christmas, so take time to share that gift with others this holiday season.

Prayer

Jesus, thank You for giving me the greatest gift of all. Help me to use Your gifts and share Your love with others. Amen.

Family Discussion Questions

» Of all of the presents you have ever received, which one is your favorite? Why?

» How do you feel when you give a gift to someone else? How would you feel if they never opened it or used it?

» Why is Jesus the greatest gift we could ever receive?

» How can we share Jesus's gift with others?

Family Adventure: Make Holiday Gifts

Make holiday gifts (*like today's peppermint bark*) and give them away to friends, neighbors, family, the elderly, the homeless, etc. with an encouraging note and reminder that Jesus is the greatest gift of all. *(Go to KatieJTrent.com/Advent for free printable templates.)*

Baking Buddies Conversation Connection

"Every good and perfect gift is from above, coming down from the Father of the heavenly lights, who does not change like shifting shadows" (James 1:17 NIV). Today we are making Pure White Chocolate Peppermint Bark to give as gifts to bless other people and remind them that Jesus is the greatest gift of all.

PURE WHITE CHOCOLATE PEPPERMINT BARK

Ingredients

24 oz. vanilla almond bark
20 regular-sized peppermint candy canes (*10 oz.*)

Directions

Cover a large rimmed baking sheet (*any size*) with parchment paper or a silicone baking mat and set aside.

Unwrap and crush the candy canes into small pieces either by pulsing in a food processor or by placing them in a large zipper bag (*push the air out before sealing*) and hitting the candy canes with the end of a rolling pin. (*Note: I recommend placing a towel over the top of the bag before crushing the candy to help prevent pieces from flying around.*)

Set aside $^1/_3$ of the candy canes in a small bowl to garnish the top of the bark.

Chop the almond bark into smaller chunks to help it melt quicker. Place the pieces in a glass or ceramic (*microwave-safe*) bowl and microwave on 50% power for 3 minutes. An *adult* should carefully take the bowl out using a towel so you don't burn yourself, and stir the mixture with a rubber spatula. Place the mixture back in the microwave and heat again at 50% power for another 30-60 seconds, or until the mixture has fully melted. (*Note: It's best to use smaller time increments and stir often so you don't burn the mixture.*)

Stir $^2/_3$ of the crushed candy canes into the mixture and then pour the mixture onto the lined baking sheet and spread into an even layer with an offset spatula.

Sprinkle the remaining $^1/_3$ of the crushed candy canes over top of the mixture.

Allow the bark to set either on the counter or in the fridge. (*It will take about an hour to fully set in the fridge, or 2-3 hours at room temperature.*)

Once the bark has fully hardened, you can either use a knife or your hands to break it into smaller pieces and place in treat bags. Write a note along with a Scripture (*I recommend John 3:16 or James 1:17*) and deliver for a sweet gift to bless others this Christmas season.

(*Makes 8 packages of 4 ½ oz. each*)

21

GENEROSITY TRANSFORMS LIVES / GIVING

Tell them to use their money to do good.
They should be rich in good works and generous to those in need,
always being ready to share with others.
—1 Timothy 6:18

Have you heard the saying, "Let's keep Christ in Christmas"? It's a common phrase this time of year, but have you thought about what it really means? How can we keep Christ in Christmas? Is it by saying "Merry Christmas" instead of "Happy holidays"? Is it by reading the story of Christ's birth in our Bibles? Or is it something more?

The Advent season leading up to Christmas is known as a time of giving. People pay more attention to the needs of those around them and look for additional ways to serve their communities. Even those who don't believe in Jesus tend to give more to charities and be more generous this time of year. Why do you think that is? How does your family give during this season?

As we celebrate the birth of Jesus, it's only fitting that we seek to give and bless others. Jesus modeled a life of selflessness and generosity for us. He loved people with His words and His actions. He was moved with compassion and reached out to the lost, hurting, and broken around Him.

Jesus also took care of the practical needs of people, like feeding the multitudes so they wouldn't have to walk home hungry. He spent His life serving others. If we want to be more like Jesus, we will live a life of service, compassion, and generosity too.

In a season where it's easy to get caught up in all the gifts, treats, and experiences that we want for ourselves, let's make sure we remember our Savior and seek to put the needs of others above ourselves. Let's live generously and love boldly. Let's invest our time, talents, and resources to make the world a better place—being sensitive to the needs of others and showing the love of Christ in practical and tangible ways.

Prayer

Jesus, thank You for showing us how to live a life of sacrificial love and generosity. Help us to be sensitive to the needs of others and spread Your love through giving and serving those around us. Amen.

Family Discussion Questions

» How did Jesus model or show generosity?

» What are some ways you could bless and help others?

» How does generosity help spread the gospel of Christ?

» What's one thing you can do today to show kindness and compassion to someone else?

Family Adventure: Spread Generosity

Spread generosity today by giving to a charity, writing a kind note to someone, serving your community together, helping a neighbor, paying for someone's meal, giving a bag of supplies to the homeless, or doing something else to show the love and compassion of Jesus.

Baking Buddies Conversation Connection

In 2 Corinthians 9:11–13, we're told:

Yes, you will be enriched in every way so that you can always be generous. And when we take your gifts to those who need them, they will thank God. So two good things will result from this ministry of giving—the needs of the believers in Jerusalem will be met, and they will joyfully express their thanks to God. As a result of your ministry, they will give glory to God. For your generosity to them and to all believers will prove that you are obedient to the Good News of Christ.

Today we're making Love of Jesus White Chocolate Pretzel Crosses or Love of Jesus Breakfast Toast (*your choice*) to help us remember to always be generous and spread the love of Jesus whenever we can.

LOVE OF JESUS WHITE CHOCOLATE PRETZEL CROSSES

Ingredients

12 oz. white chocolate melting wafers
20 pretzel rods
Red sprinkles or sanding sugar, optional

Directions

Cover a large baking sheet with wax paper or a silicone baking mat. Set aside.

Cut 3 or 4 pretzel rods into 1" pieces *(you will use two for each cross you make)*.

Melt white chocolate wafers in a microwave-safe glass mug according to the package directions.

Use tongs to dip a full pretzel rod into the chocolate *(you can coat both sides or leave the bottom of the rod uncoated)*. Lay covered pretzel rod on the prepared baking sheet.

Quickly dip two of the 1" pretzel pieces into the white chocolate and press them on each side of the long pretzel to form the shape of a cross.

Sprinkle with sanding sugar or sprinkles if desired.

Continue until you've made as many pretzel crosses as you want.

(Remind your kids that Jesus gave His life for us because He loves us and wants a relationship with us. And as we celebrate His birth, we remember His sacrifice for us on the cross.)

LOVE OF JESUS BREAKFAST TOAST

Ingredients (*per person*)

1 egg
1 slice of bread
1 tbsp. unsalted butter
Pinch of salt
Pinch of pepper

Additional items needed:

Heart-shaped cookie cutter (*or knife to cut heart shapes*)

Directions

Use the cookie cutter or a knife to cut out a heart shape from the middle of the slice of bread.

Heat a frying pan or griddle to medium heat. Then melt the butter over the heated surface.

Add the bread to the pan or griddle.

Carefully crack the egg into the heart-shaped middle of the bread. Sprinkle with salt and pepper and allow it to cook for about a minute.

Use a spatula to carefully flip the toast over to cook on the other side for another minute (*or until the egg is cooked to your liking*).

Serve and enjoy.

22

WHITE AS SNOW / COLORS OF CHRISTMAS

"Come now, let's settle this," says the LORD.
"Though your sins are like scarlet, I will make them as white as snow.
Though they are red like crimson, I will make them as white as wool."
—Isaiah 1:18

God created a world filled with beautiful colors. What colors do you think of when you hear the word *Christmas?* Red? Green? There are many colors associated with the Christmas season—red, white, green, gold, silver, and blue are probably the most common. Why do you think we connect certain colors with certain holidays, such as brown, orange, red, and yellow for Thanksgiving, or red and pink for Valentine's Day?

Colors can remind us of many things. Green is often equated with new life and growth, like fresh leaves sprouting. White is known for purity, just as the prophet Isaiah tells us that Jesus washes away our sins and makes them as white as snow. Red reminds us of the blood of Jesus. What else do you think of when you see the colors of Christmas? How do these colors make you feel?

Whenever you see the colors of Christmas, remember Jesus shed His blood for us, washing away our sins and giving us a new life in Him. Second Corinthians 5:17 (NKJV) says, *"Therefore, if anyone is in Christ, he is a new creation; old things have passed away; behold, all things have become new."* Thank Jesus for His love and sacrifice whenever you see the colors of Christmas.

Prayer

Jesus, thank You for giving me new life in You. Help me to remember Your sacrifice and live a life that honors You. Amen.

Family Discussion Questions

» What's your favorite color and why?

» Which color of Christmas means the most to you? Why?

» Why do you think colors are so important?

» What does it mean when the Bible says in Isaiah 1:18, *"Though your sins are like scarlet, I will make them as white as snow"*?

Family Adventure: Christmas Coloring

Color Christmas pictures. Draw your own using the colors of Christmas, or simply print coloring pages. You'll also find some printable coloring pages at KatieJTrent.com/Advent.

Baking Buddies Conversation Connection

Psalm 51:7 says, *"Purify me from my sins, and I will be clean; wash me, and I will be whiter than snow."* Today we're making Wash Me Whiter Than Snow Christmas Punch or Wash Me Whiter Than Snow Kiwi Strawberry Yogurt Parfaits *(your choice)* to remind us that when we ask

Jesus for forgiveness, He forgives our sins and washes us whiter than snow. The red and green colors help us to remember that we have new life in Christ because of the blood He shed for us on the cross.

WASH ME WHITER THAN SNOW CHRISTMAS PUNCH

Ingredients

½ cup granulated sugar

¼ cup hot water

3 oz. (*6 tbsp.*) evaporated milk

½ - 1 tsp. almond extract (*can substitute with clear vanilla extract if desired*)

½ gallon vanilla ice cream

1 (2 liter) bottle of lemon-lime soda, chilled

*Top with whipped cream and red/green sprinkles

Directions

Combine sugar and water in a small glass (*microwave-safe*) bowl. Heat for 30 seconds in the microwave to dissolve the sugar. (*Note: If you want the punch to be less sweet, you can skip the sugar and water and proceed to the next step instead*)

Stir in the evaporated milk and almond extract (*for a lighter almond flavor, use ½ tsp. of almond extract instead of 1 tsp. or substitute with clear vanilla extract if you prefer*).

Pour mixture into a large punch bowl and add the vanilla ice cream. Use a potato masher to break the ice cream into small chunks.

Carefully stir in the soda. Ladle punch into individual cups and top with whipped cream and sprinkles to bring together all the colors of Christmas.

WASH ME WHITER THAN SNOW KIWI STRAWBERRY YOGURT PARFAITS

Ingredients

32 oz. Greek vanilla yogurt (*you can use regular yogurt or dairy-free if desired*)
4 kiwis, peeled and diced (*if you don't have kiwis, you can substitute with sliced green grapes or green apples instead*)
1 pint strawberries, hulled and diced (*keep 4 strawberries whole to garnish glasses if desired*)
2 tbsp. honey
2 cups prepared granola
Note: *You can substitute red and green apples instead of kiwi and strawberry if you prefer.*

Additional items needed:

4 clear cups or parfait jars

Directions

Add 2 tablespoons of granola into the bottoms of each parfait cup. Set aside.

In a medium bowl, stir together the diced strawberries and kiwi (*or other fruit*).

Add the honey to the fruit and stir to combine. Set aside.

Spoon a layer of yogurt over top of the granola in each parfait cup and then add a layer of fruit.

Add another layer of granola, yogurt, and fruit.

Sprinkle the tops with granola and then garnish with a whole strawberry (*if desired*).

Serve and enjoy.

23

JESUS DESERVES OUR BEST / WISE MEN

Jesus was born in Bethlehem in Judea, during the reign of King Herod. About that time some wise men from eastern lands arrived in Jerusalem, asking, "Where is the newborn king of the Jews? We saw his star as it rose, and we have come to worship him."... They entered the house and saw the child with his mother, Mary, and they bowed down and worshiped him. Then they opened their treasure chests and gave him gifts of gold, frankincense, and myrrh.

—Matthew 2:1–2, 11

The wise men, also known as the magi, are an important part of the Christmas story. Why do you think they're referred to as *wise men*? What do we know about them from the Bible? We don't know for sure how many wise men traveled to visit Jesus, but we do know that they brought three specific gifts to celebrate Jesus's birth. Do you remember what they were?

The three gifts the wise men brought were gold, frankincense, and myrrh. Why do you think they brought those specific gifts to Jesus? They

204 A Merry and Bright Adventure

weren't the most practical gifts to give a baby. What would you bring to a baby today? What gifts would you have given to Jesus?

Many say the three gifts represented Jesus's royalty, divinity, and humanity.[12] They were the very best gifts those wise men could bring. They wanted to honor Jesus, the newborn King of the Jews.

The wise men remind us that Jesus deserves our very best too. But how do we do that? We can put Jesus first in our lives by praying to Him regularly, seeking His wisdom and His will as we make decisions, and by honoring Him with our time, our talents, and our treasure.

Prayer

Jesus, help us to be wise and to always give our best to You and those around us. Amen.

Family Discussion Questions

- » What gift would you bring Jesus if you met Him today?

- » How can you honor Jesus this Christmas season?

- » What can you do to give Jesus your best all year long?

- » If you could only receive one gift from God, what would you want it to be? Why?

Family Adventure:
Play the 3 Gifts for Jesus Game

To play the game, set a timer for five minutes and have everyone run around the house to collect three things they would give Jesus if they were the wise men. Come back together and share what you chose and why.

12. Alfred Edersheim, "Why Gold, Frankincense, and Myrrh?", *Christianity.com*, November 17, 2023, www.christianity.com/jesus/birth-of-jesus/star-and-magi/why-gold-frankincense-and-myrrh.html.

Then talk about gifts we can give Jesus every day (*our time, our talents, and our treasure*).

Baking Buddies Conversation Connection

The wise men brought three gifts for Jesus, so today we're making Wise Men White Chocolate Popcorn Gifts to give to others. God's Word says:

> *For you know that God paid a ransom to save you from the empty life you inherited from your ancestors. And it was not paid with mere gold or silver, which lose their value. It was the precious blood of Christ, the sinless, spotless Lamb of God.* (1 Peter 1:18–19)

The popcorn is white, which reminds us that Jesus was the pure and spotless Lamb of God. He was without sin, yet He died for our sins so we could spend eternity with Him in heaven. White chocolate covers the popcorn and binds it together, which reminds us that when we accept Jesus as our Lord and Savior, He covers our sins, washes them white as snow, and seals us with the Holy Spirit forever. (*See, respectively, Isaiah 1:18; Ephesians 1:13.*)

The red candies remind us that Jesus redeemed us with His blood when He died on the cross for our sins, while the green candies remind us that we are new creations in Christ Jesus. (*See, respectively, Ephesians 1:7; 2 Corinthians 5:17.*) Finally, the sprinkles remind us to spread the good news of the gospel everywhere we go, sprinkling our words and actions with the love of Christ.

WISE MEN WHITE CHOCOLATE POPCORN GIFTS

Ingredients

2 bags white popcorn, not buttered (*8 cups popped popcorn*)
12 oz. white chocolate candy melts
10 oz. red and green chocolate candies
Red and green Christmas sprinkles

Additional items needed:

Microwave
Treat bags or zipper sandwich bags
Rimmed baking sheet & parchment paper or baking mat

Directions

Use the microwave to pop one bag of popcorn at a time, per the directions on the bags.

Prepare a rimmed baking sheet with parchment paper or a baking mat and set aside.

Scoop the popped kernels into a large bowl, making sure to remove any unpopped kernels.

Sprinkle the candies over the popcorn.

Use a microwave-safe bowl to melt the vanilla or white chocolate candy melts on 50% power 30 seconds at a time, stirring after each interval until the candy melts are smooth.

Carefully drizzle half of the candy melts over the top of the popcorn mixture. Use a rubber spatula to stir the mixture and gently toss it a few times, then sprinkle with Christmas sprinkles.

Drizzle the remaining candy melts over the popcorn and quickly toss with spatula again to evenly coat.

Pour out the covered popcorn into an even layer on your prepared baking sheet and quickly sprinkle with sprinkles again before the white chocolate hardens.

Allow the mixture to cool and then gently break into chunks.

For gifts, place a few chunks in small treat bags or zipper sandwich bags to seal. Write a nice note and deliver to family, friends, or neighbors— or simply enjoy the treat together as a family. (*Makes 8 cups*)

24

THE BREAD OF LIFE / CHRISTMAS DINNER

Look! I stand at the door and knock. If you hear my voice and open the door, I will come in, and we will share a meal together as friends.
—Revelation 3:20

The Bible talks about food a lot, which kind of makes me hungry sometimes. How about you? Did you know that Jesus frequently shared meals with strangers and friends? Why do you think that is mentioned so often in the Bible? He fed the large crowds of people who followed Him and encouraged us to look after the poor and needy too. He even instructed us to feed our enemies. Have you ever fed someone who was really mean to you? It can be hard, but as Christians, we are taught to love our enemies and bless those who hurt us.

Some of the most important events in the Bible are remembered through large feasts. Can you think of any? *(Feasts of Passover, Unleavened Bread, First Fruits, Harvest, Trumpets, Day of Atonement, and Tabernacles.)* In fact, the last thing Jesus did with His disciples before He went to the cross was to share the Passover meal with them. He encouraged us as believers to remember Him whenever we take communion. Have you ever taken communion?

Christmas dinner is a special time to remember Jesus and all He has done for us. Some families gather with their extended family or friends for this meal. Others invite strangers or people who are lonely into their homes to share Christmas dinner with them. What does your family do? Do you have any special foods or traditions you enjoy for this special occasion?

Jesus told His followers, *"I am the bread of life. Whoever comes to me will never be hungry again. Whoever believes in me will never be thirsty"* (John 6:35). What do you think Jesus meant by this?

Whatever you do for Christmas dinner this year, be sure to take time to remember Jesus and all He's done for you and your family. Celebrate His life and the eternal life He made available to you.

Prayer

Jesus, thank You for giving me eternal life. Help me to remember that You are all I need. Please help me love generously and feed those around me—even my enemies. Amen.

Family Discussion Questions

» Why does Jesus refer to Himself as the *bread of life?*

» Why do you think so much of Jesus's ministry involved food?

» What is your favorite part of Christmas dinner?

» Who could you invite to share a meal with you?

Family Adventure: Take Communion Together

Take communion together as a family. You can use bread or crackers along with juice, water, etc., or pre-packaged communion cups. (*Note: Today's recipe is unleavened bread you can use for communion if you wish.*)

In 1 Corinthians 11:23–26, Paul says:

For I pass on to you what I received from the Lord himself. On the night when he was betrayed, the Lord Jesus took some bread and gave thanks to God for it. Then he broke it in pieces and said, "This is my body, which is given for you. Do this in remembrance of me." In the same way, he took the cup of wine after supper, saying, "This cup is the new covenant between God and his people—an agreement confirmed with my blood. Do this in remembrance of me as often as you drink it." For every time you eat this bread and drink this cup, you are announcing the Lord's death until he comes again.

Baking Buddies Conversation Connection

After Jesus returned to heaven, His believers *"worshiped together at the Temple each day, met in homes for the Lord's Supper, and shared their meals with great joy and generosity"* (Acts 2:46). Today we're making Unleavened Bread of Life to remind us that Jesus is the daily bread we need to sustain us each and every day.

UNLEAVENED BREAD OF LIFE

Ingredients

2 cups flour, plus 2 tbsp. for rolling *(may substitute 1:1 gluten-free baking flour if desired)*
1 cup cold water
½ tsp. kosher salt

Additional items needed:

Rolling pin
Stovetop & skillet
Can use butter & cinnamon/sugar for bread if desired

Directions

In a medium bowl, combine 2 cups flour and salt.

Stir in the water with a wooden spoon until the dough comes together in a ball.

Use clean hands to knead the dough for 5 minutes by pushing the dough away from you with the heel of your palm and then folding it over itself and pulling it back.

Preheat a large skillet on medium-low heat.

Divide the dough into 6-7 equal pieces and roll into balls with your hands.

Lightly flour a surface to roll out the dough with the remaining 2 tbsp. of flour. Use a rolling pin to roll each ball flat until it's about 6" in diameter.

Cook each piece in the skillet one at a time for approximately two minutes on each side, then remove from heat.

Enjoy the bread warm or cooled. It's perfect for communion or as a treat with butter and cinnamon/sugar.

25

PRAISE TO THE LORD / NATIVITY SCENE

At that time the Roman emperor, Augustus, decreed that a census should be taken throughout the Roman Empire. (This was the first census taken when Quirinius was governor of Syria.) All returned to their own ancestral towns to register for this census. And because Joseph was a descendant of King David, he had to go to Bethlehem in Judea, David's ancient home. He traveled there from the village of Nazareth in Galilee. He took with him Mary, to whom he was engaged, who was now expecting a child. And while they were there, the time came for her baby to be born. She gave birth to her firstborn son. She wrapped him snugly in strips of cloth and laid him in a manger, because there was no lodging available for them. That night there were shepherds staying in the fields nearby, guarding their flocks of sheep. Suddenly, an angel of the Lord appeared among them, and the radiance of the Lord's glory surrounded them. They were terrified, but the angel reassured them. "Don't be afraid!" he said. "I bring you good news that will bring great joy to all people. The Savior—yes, the Messiah, the Lord—has been born today in Bethlehem, the city of David! And you will recognize him by this sign: You will find a baby wrapped snugly in strips of cloth, lying in a manger."
Suddenly, the angel was joined by a vast host of others—the armies of heaven—praising God and saying, "Glory to God in highest heaven,

and peace on earth to those with whom God is pleased." When the
angels had returned to heaven, the shepherds said to each other, "Let's
go to Bethlehem! Let's see this thing that has happened, which the
Lord has told us about." They hurried to the village and found Mary
and Joseph. And there was the baby, lying in the manger. After seeing
him, the shepherds told everyone what had happened and what the
angel had said to them about this child.
—Luke 2:1–17

Merry Christmas! This is the long-awaited day! And while we didn't have to wait over four hundred years like the Israelites did, it might have felt like it at times. We've spent the past four weeks preparing our hearts for this day. How does it feel?

One of the most iconic symbols of Christmas is the nativity scene. They come in all shapes and sizes, and typically feature Mary, Joseph, and baby Jesus in a manger with wise men or shepherds. Nativity sets are meant to capture the reason we celebrate Christmas: to honor the birth of our Lord and Savior, Jesus Christ.

Now that we've learned how all the sights and sounds of the Christmas season point us toward Jesus, we can set out to discover how the world around us each day can also draw us closer to Him. We learn more about our Creator by observing and studying His creation. It's super amazing to think that the God who created the heavens and the earth also uniquely formed and created each of us. Even better is knowing that He has great plans for our lives.

The truth is, we're not here by accident, but by divine design. God has called and created us for such a time as this. And the more we search Him out, the stronger our relationship with Him will be. Jeremiah 29:13 (NKJV) says, *"You will seek Me and find Me, when you search for Me with all your heart."* So, keep your eyes on Jesus today and every day. Remember, He loves you so much that He sacrificed His life so you could spend eternity with Him.

Prayer

God, thank You for sending Jesus to earth for us. Thank You for loving us and inviting us to spend eternity with You. Help us to live for You each day and fulfill our purpose on earth. Amen.

Family Discussion Questions

» Why is Christmas such a special time of year?

» How can you honor Jesus today?

» How can you build a stronger relationship with Jesus?

» What can you do to love like Jesus today?

Family Adventure: Pray

Take time to pray together as a family and thank Jesus for all He's done for you. Talk about ways you can focus on—and live for—Jesus daily. For fun, snap a picture of your family with this book and share on social media how *A Merry and Bright Adventure* has impacted your life. Be sure to tag me @KatieJTrent and #KatieJTrentAdventures so I can celebrate with you!

Baking Buddies Conversation Connection

With its sweet aroma, cinnamon is a familiar scent at Christmastime. It is even mentioned several times throughout the Bible. (For example, *Exodus 30:23, Revelation 18:13.*) In one of his psalms, David says, "O LORD, I am calling to you. Please hurry! Listen when I cry to you for help! Accept my prayer as incense offered to you, and my upraised hands as an evening offering" (Psalm

141:1–2). Today we're making a sweet-smelling recipe to help us remember to continually pray and offer our worship as a sweet-smelling sacrifice to God: Christmas Morning Cinnamon Bread or Christmas Slow-Cooker Cinnamon Apple Cider (*your choice*).

CHRISTMAS MORNING CINNAMON BREAD

Ingredients

2 cups granulated sugar
4 cups all-purpose flour
2 tbsp. baking powder
1 tsp. kosher salt
2 large eggs
2 cups milk *(or milk alternative)*
⅔ cup oil *(vegetable, avocado, canola, etc.)*

Topping:

4 tsp. cinnamon
⅔ cup granulated sugar

Optional glaze:

1 ½ cups powdered sugar, sifted
3-5 tbsp. milk, heavy cream, or milk alternative
½ tsp. pure vanilla extract

Directions

Preheat oven to 350 degrees.

Grease 2 regular-sized *(1 lb.)* loaf pans and set aside.

In a medium bowl, combine sugar, flour, baking powder, and salt. Whisk to combine and set aside.

In a large mixing bowl, whisk together eggs, milk, and oil.

Gradually add the dry ingredients to the wet ones, combining just until moist. *(Don't overmix)*.

Pour half of the mixture into each prepared loaf pan *(approximately ⅔ full)*.

In a small bowl, combine the cinnamon and ⅔ cup sugar and stir together.

Spoon some of the cinnamon/sugar topping on each loaf and use a butter knife to gently swirl it into the loaf, leaving some on top.

Bake for 40-50 minutes, until a toothpick inserted into the center comes out clean. Allow loaves to cool for 10 minutes before turning them out onto wire racks. Enjoy warm or serve once they've cooled. Top with glaze if desired.

To make optional glaze:

Sift powdered sugar into a medium-sized bowl.

Add vanilla extract and one tablespoon of milk or milk alternative and whisk to combine. Continue adding one tablespoon of milk at a time until you reach the desired consistency *(should be able to drizzle it over the finished loaves without it being too runny)*.

CHRISTMAS SLOW-COOKER CINNAMON APPLE CIDER

Ingredients

64 oz. apple cider
6 chai tea bags
2 cinnamon sticks *(or 2 tsp. ground cinnamon)*
1 vanilla bean, split *(Alternative: 1 tsp. vanilla bean paste or pure vanilla extract)*
¼ cup lemon juice
**Apple slices and/or cinnamon sticks for serving, if desired*

Directions

Combine apple cider, chai tea bags, cinnamon, and vanilla in slow cooker.

Cook on low heat for 3-4 hours.

Discard tea bags.

Stir in lemon juice and serve warm. Add an apple slice or cinnamon stick to glass for decoration if desired.

APPENDICES

GROCERY SHOPPING LISTS

Note: Parchment paper or silicone baking mats will be used frequently throughout the month, and you will either need a kitchen stand mixer or an electric hand mixer for many of the recipes, along with cookie cutters (hearts, stars, letters, and holiday shapes) and other common baking utensils. Less common non-food items that you may need to grab are listed in bold.

SECTION ONE: HOPE

Day 1: What's the Fruit? Smoothie Ingredients

3 cups frozen fruit *(or fruit mix)* of choice
1 ¼ cup milk *(or milk alternative)*
½ cup Greek yogurt or nut butter of choice
Straws

Day 2: Starry Grilled Cheese Sandwiches (or your child's favorite sandwich) Ingredients

2 slices of bread per person
1-2 slices of cheese per person
3-4 tbsp. butter
If making alternative sandwich, have ingredients needed for them
Star-shaped cookie cutter (1" to 3" will work)

Day 3: Picasso Puzzle Pancakes Ingredients

1 ¼ cup flour *(can use flour of choice; may substitute gluten-free 1:1 baking flour)*

2 ½ - 3 tsp. baking powder

2 tbsp. granulated sugar

¾ tsp. salt

1 large egg

1 ¼ cup milk *(or milk alternative)*

3 tbsp. oil *(canola, vegetable, olive, avocado, etc.)*

Butter or oil spray to grease pan

Gel food coloring or natural ingredients like matcha, freeze-dried fruit, turmeric, etc. to dye batter *(if desired, not necessary)*

Toppings Ideas *(choose what you want)*:

Maple syrup

Fresh fruit

Nut butter

Sprinkles

Whipped topping

Chocolate chips

Different shaped cookie cutters *(if desired)*

Day 4: Don't be a Grinch Christmas Punch Ingredients

½ gallon lime sherbet

1 liter lemon-lime soda

½ gallon green Hawaiian fruit punch *(or lemon-lime Kool-Aid package and 1 cup granulated sugar)*

Red sanding sugar to line the cup rims *(if desired)*

Note: *If you want a healthier alternative, you can make anything green for today, like a salad, cucumber or celery slices, green smoothie, etc.*

Day 5: Sealed-With-A-Bow Puff Pastry Treat Ingredients

1 pkg. puff pastry dough

1 egg white

1 cup powdered sugar

½ lemon *(will use zest & juice)* or you can use 1-2 tsp. of vanilla extract if you prefer

¼ cup chopped almonds *(for nut alternatives, try pumpkin or sunflower seeds or chopped pretzels instead)*

For glaze:

1 cup powered sugar

Vanilla extract

1-3 tbsp. milk of your choice

Day 6: Sweet Santa Hat Strawberries

8 oz. cream cheese

½ cup powdered sugar

½ tsp. pure vanilla extract

1 pint fresh strawberries

2-3 bananas

20 lollipop sticks (or toothpicks without sharp points)

SECTION TWO: PEACE/PREPARATION

Day 7: Better Than Birdfeed Trail Mix Ingredients

2 cups dry roasted peanuts, almonds, or nut mix of choice *(for nut allergies, utilize popcorn, cereal, or other crunchy/salty item of choice)*

1 cup chocolate covered pretzels

1 cup mini holiday chocolate coated candies

½ cup semi-sweet chocolate chips

½ cup white chocolate chips

½ cup raisins, dried fruit, etc. *(if desired to cut the sweetness)*

Day 8: Fill Your Heart with Good Fruit Pie Ingredients

2 frozen pie crust rounds *(or make your own pie dough)*

12 tsp. jam or preserves *(use 2-3 types of jam so your kids can choose a flavor to fill their pies with)*

1 egg
1 tbsp. milk or milk alternative
¼ cup sanding sugar (*any color*)
¼ cup flour to roll dough
3" heart-shaped cookie cutter
Rolling pin
Basting brush

Day 9: Salt & Light Salted Caramel Cookie Bars Ingredients

1 cup (*2 sticks*) unsalted butter
1 cup light brown sugar
½ cup granulated sugar
2 large eggs
1 tsp. vanilla extract
2 ½ cups all-purpose flour (*may substitute gluten-free 1:1 baking flour*)
1 tsp. kosher salt
1 tsp. baking soda
2 cups semi-sweet chocolate chips
14 oz. sweetened condensed milk (*or sweetened condensed coconut milk*)
10 oz. soft caramels
1 tsp. flaked sea salt
Nonstick cooking spray or butter to grease pan

Day 10: Worth the Wait Slow-Cooker Peppermint Hot Cocoa Ingredients

2 cups heavy cream
5 ½ cups whole milk
14 oz. sweetened condensed milk
1 tsp. peppermint extract
3 cups (high quality) milk chocolate chips
Toppings (*if desired*):
Mini marshmallows

Mini candy canes

Whipped cream

Note: *If you want to make the healthier alternative recipe instead (Fun Fruit Canes), you'll need a pint of fresh strawberries, a banana for each person, and a spread to bind the fruit together (nut butter, hazelnut spread, or yogurt).*

Day 11: Merry Christmas Cookies (*2 recipes to choose from*)

Gingerbread Cookie Ingredients

¾ cup unsalted butter (*1 ½ sticks*)

¾ cup dark brown sugar

⅔ cup molasses

1 large egg

1 tsp. pure vanilla extract

3 ¼ cup all-purpose flour (*may substitute gluten-free 1:1 baking flour*)

1 tbsp. ground ginger

1 tsp. baking soda

1 tsp. ground cinnamon

½ tsp. ground cloves

¼ tsp. ground nutmeg

½ tsp. kosher salt

Sugar cookie icing to decorate with

Cookie cutter letters to spell "Merry Christmas" and other holiday shapes

Gel food coloring to dye icing (*if desired*)

Sugar Cookie Ingredients

1 cup unsalted butter (*2 sticks*)

1 cup granulated sugar

1 large egg

1 tbsp. milk

3 cups all-purpose flour (*may substitute gluten-free 1:1 baking flour*)

¾ tsp. baking powder

¼ tsp. salt

Powdered sugar for rolling out dough

Sugar cookie icing to decorate with
Cookie cutter letters to spell "Merry Christmas" and other holiday shapes
Gel food coloring to dye icing *(if desired)*
Royal Icing Ingredients *(if you want to make your own instead of buying sugar cookie icing or frosting for cookies)*
4 cups powdered sugar
3 tbsp. meringue powder
9 tbsp. water
Gel food coloring to dye icing *(if desired)*

Day 12: Red Raspberry Peaceful Poinsettia Fluff Ingredients

1 pkg. (*4.6 oz.*) cook and serve vanilla pudding (*not instant*)
1 pkg. (*6 oz.*) raspberry jello mix
2 cups water
1 tsp. lemon juice
16 oz. whipped topping
2 cups raspberries (fresh or frozen)

SECTION THREE: JOY

Day 13: Light of the World Krispie Trees Ingredients

9 cups crisped rice cereal
9 cups mini marshmallows
6 tbsp. butter
Green gel food coloring
White melting chocolate wafers (*or can of white frosting*)
Star-shaped sprinkles
Mini candies (*if desired*) for decorating
2 round (8") cake pans

Day 14: Angels French Toast Ingredients

1 angel food cake (full-sized round cake)

3 large eggs
¾ cup milk (or milk alternative)
1 tbsp. flour
2 tsp. vanilla extract
¼ tsp. salt
¼ tsp. cinnamon
3-5 tbsp. butter or nonstick cooking spray to grease pan
Topping Ideas:
Maple syrup
Whipped cream
Fresh fruit (strawberries, blueberries, etc.)

Day 15: (*2 recipes to choose from*)

Bananas-About-You Fruit Candles Ingredients
8 bananas
16 oz. pre-cut cantaloupe chunks (*or cut your own*)
8 strawberries
½ cup lemon juice
16 mini chocolate chips (*or candy eyes*)
¼ cup cylinder-shaped chocolate sprinkles (*for mouth and wick*)
1" biscuit cutter or circle cookie cutter
Light the Way Confetti Cupcakes Ingredients
3 cups all-purpose flour
1 ½ tsp. baking powder
¾ tsp. salt
1 ¾ cup granulated sugar
4 eggs
¾ cup vegetable, avocado, or canola oil
1 cup milk (or milk alternative)
1 tbsp. pure vanilla extract
½ cup rainbow (rod-like) sprinkles + extra for top
24 regular-sized paper cupcake liners
2 muffin/cupcake pans (12 cups per pan)
Birthday candles

Note: You can also buy a box of confetti cake mix and 2 cans of frosting and make the cupcakes according to the package instructions.
Frosting Ingredients
½ cup (*1 stick*) unsalted butter
8 oz. cream cheese
2-3 cups powdered sugar
1 tbsp. milk
1 ½ tsp. lemon juice
½ tsp. lemon zest

Day 16: Wrapped Like Jesus (*choose peanut butter and jelly, turkey and cheese, or scrambled eggs and cheese*)

Flour tortillas (enough for your family)
Fillings of choice:
*Peanut butter and jelly or honey
*Lunch meat and cheese, mustard and mayonnaise
*Scrambled eggs and cheese

Day 17: Mom's Cheerful Chocolate Chip Cookies Ingredients

4 ½ cups all-purpose flour
2 tsp. baking soda
2 tsp. kosher salt
2 cups (2 sticks) butter-flavored shortening (**Note:** *You can use butter instead, but I highly recommend the shortening sticks for the perfect texture and flavor—they are the secret ingredient to the perfect cookies*)
1 ½ cups granulated sugar
1 ½ cups brown sugar
2 tsp. pure vanilla extract
4 large eggs
2 cups (12 oz. pkg.) semi-sweet chocolate chips
2 cups (12 oz. pkg.) white chocolate chips

Day 18: Cranberry Christmas Carol Cake Ingredients

3 eggs

2 cups granulated sugar

¾ cup unsalted butter

1 tsp. pure vanilla extract

2 cups all-purpose flour (may substitute gluten-free 1:1 baking flour)

12 oz. fresh or frozen cranberries

SECTION FOUR: LOVE

Day 19: (*2 recipes to choose from*)

Wrapped in God's Love Hotdog Wreaths Ingredients

1 tube refrigerated crescent roll dough

24 miniature hotdogs

¼ cup Dijon mustard

1 egg

Splash of milk (*or milk alternative*)

Sprinkle of salt

Rosemary sprigs for decoration (*optional*)

Ketchup and/or mustard (*for dipping*)

Sealed with God Marshmallow Wreaths Ingredients

4 cups mini marshmallows

½ cup salted butter

1 tsp. green gel food coloring

½ tsp. pure vanilla extract

½ tsp. almond extract

4 cups cornflake cereal

2 ¼ oz. cinnamon red hot candies

1" – 2" round biscuit or cookie cutter

Day 20: Pure White Chocolate Peppermint Bark Ingredients

24 oz. vanilla almond bark
20 regular-sized peppermint candy canes *(10 oz.)*

Day 21: *(2 recipes to choose from)*

Love of Jesus White Chocolate Pretzel Cross Ingredients
12 oz. white chocolate melting wafers
20 pretzel rods
Red sprinkles or sanding sugar *(optional)*
Love of Jesus Breakfast Toast Ingredients *(per person)*
1 egg
1 slice of bread
1 tbsp. unsalted butter
Pinch of salt
Pinch of pepper
Heart-shaped cookie cutter or knife to cut heart shape out of bread

Day 22: *(2 recipes to choose from)*

Wash Me Whiter Than Snow Christmas Punch Ingredients
½ cup sugar
¼ cup hot water
3 oz. evaporated milk
½ - 1 tsp. almond extract (or clear vanilla extract)
½ gallon vanilla ice cream
2-liter bottle of lemon-lime soda
Optional toppings:
Whipped cream
Red and green sprinkles
Wash Me Whiter Than Snow Kiwi Strawberry Yogurt Parfait Ingredients
32 oz. Greek vanilla yogurt *(you can use regular yogurt or dairy-free if desired)*

4 kiwis, peeled and diced (*if you don't have kiwis, you can substitute with sliced green grapes or green apples instead*)
1 pint strawberries
2 tbsp. honey
2 cups prepared granola
4 clear cups or parfait jars

Day 23: Wise Men White Chocolate Popcorn Gift Ingredients

2 bags white popcorn (*8 cups popped popcorn, not buttered*)
12 oz. white chocolate candy melts
10 oz. red and green chocolate candies
Red and green Christmas sprinkles
Treat bags or zipper sandwich bags

Day 24: Unleavened Bread of Life Ingredients

2 cups + 2 tbsp. all-purpose flour (*or substitute gluten-free 1:1 baking flour*)
1 cup cold water
½ tsp. kosher salt
Optional: butter, cinnamon, and sugar

Day 25: (*2 recipes to choose from*)

Christmas Morning Cinnamon Bread Ingredients
2 ⅔ cups granulated sugar
4 cups all-purpose flour (*may substitute gluten-free 1:1 baking flour*)
2 tbsp. baking powder
1 tsp. kosher salt
2 large eggs
2 cups milk (*or milk alternative*)
⅔ cup oil (*vegetable, avocado, canola, etc.*)
4 tsp. cinnamon
2 loaf pans (1 lb.)
Optional Glaze Ingredients

1 ½ cups powdered sugar

3-5 tbsp. milk, heavy cream, or milk alternative

½ tsp. pure vanilla extract

Christmas Slow-Cooker Cinnamon Apple Cider Ingredients

64 oz. apple cider

6 chai tea bags

2 cinnamon sticks *(plus more to garnish cups if desired; can substitute ground cinnamon)*

1 vanilla bean *(or 1 tsp. vanilla bean paste or pure vanilla extract)*

¼ cup lemon juice

Apple slices to garnish cups *(if desired)*

FAMILY ADVENTURE SUPPLY LISTS

Art Supplies to Keep on Hand

- » Construction paper
- » White cardstock
- » White printer paper
- » Markers/colored pencils/crayons
- » Kid scissors
- » Glue sticks
- » Glue
- » String, twine, or ribbons for ornaments
- » Single hole punch
- » Cookie cutters (stars, hearts, circles, letters, and holiday shapes)

Note: Be sure to download and print my free complimentary Advent bundle filled with templates and other printables at KatieJTrent.com/Advent.

SECTION ONE: HOPE

DAY 1: HOPE ORNAMENTS

Construction paper, cardboard, or cardstock
Hope ornament template (*from KatieJTrent.com/Advent*)

Scissors

Markers, crayons, or colored pencils

Hole punch

String, twine, or ribbon to hang ornaments

Note: *You can also purchase prepackaged ornament crafts to design if desired and write HOPE on them*

DAY 2: FOLLOWING THE LIGHT OF JESUS FLASHLIGHT WALK

Flashlight *(walk can be inside with lights off or outside at night)*

DAY 3: MESS INTO A MESSAGE ABSTRACT ART PROJECT

Black marker or pen

White paper

Crayons, markers, or colored pencils

Image of Pablo Picasso's paintings *(like "Three Musicians," or "Still Life")*

DAY 4: MAKE AND SEND CHRISTMAS CARDS

Note: *If you prefer, you can purchase a package of pre-designed Christmas cards or have personalized photo Christmas cards on hand instead of making your own.*

White cardstock for the cards

A9 (5.75 by 8.75 inch) white peel and stick envelopes

Crayons, markers, or colored pencils

Christmas stickers *(if desired)*

Stamps for mailing

Note: *If you have young children, you can pre-print some Bible verses or sayings like "Merry Christmas" and "Love the ____ Family" or "Merry Christmas from our family to yours!" for kids to glue into cards if they can't write well yet. You'll need a glue stick as well.*

DAY 5: MAKE DECORATIVE CROSS GIFTS

Note: *You can purchase pre-made cross crafts from wood, scratch art paper, etc. if desired*
Cardstock or popsicle sticks to make the crosses
Markers, crayons, or colored pencils
Single hole punch
Stickers, jewels, etc. *(if desired)*
Red ribbon for hanging *(goes with the theme of the chapter)*
Glue if using popsicle sticks or jewels that need glued on

DAY 6: SPREAD CHRISTMAS HOPE LIKE ST. NICHOLAS

Make and deliver gift baskets, pay someone's bill, shovel snow, donate clothes and toys, etc.

SECTION TWO: PEACE/PREPARATION

DAY 7: PINE CONE BIRD FEEDERS

1 pine cone per person
1 jar peanut butter (or alternative nut butter)
Small bag of birdseed
Paper plates
String or twine (cut into 12" pieces)
Plastic butter knives or popsicle sticks for spreading

DAY 8: MAKE YOUR OWN STOCKINGS AND/OR PLAY THE FILL-YOUR-STOCKING GAME

Note: *You can use premade stockings to play the game or make your own with the following items:*
Construction paper
String
Hole punch

Markers/crayons/colored pencils
Stickers *(if desired)*

DAY 9: ENJOY A HOLIDAY LIGHT DISPLAY

Drive or walk around to enjoy holiday lights around your community

DAY 10: MAKE PIPE CLEANER CANDY CANES

Red and white pipe cleaners *(enough for each person)*
Note: *If you don't want to use pipe cleaners, you can draw or print a candy cane coloring page or make one with construction paper.*

DAY 11: IMPART A CHRISTMAS BLESSING

A Bible to find verses and promises
Paper and writing utensil to write out the blessings

DAY 12: MAKE OR PURCHASE A POINSETTIA

Refer to my printed Advent bundle for poinsettia craft ideas or purchase a poinsettia plant
For the craft, you'll need paper, glue, and coloring utensils or red and green pipe cleaners

SECTION THREE: JOY

DAY 13: STARGAZING

Head outside to gaze at the stars or sit around the twinkling lights on your Christmas tree

DAY 14: MAKE AN ANGEL CRAFT OR BLESS SOMEONE

Angel craft templates *(from KatieJTrent.com/Advent)*

Depending on which craft you choose, you may need: white paper plates, coffee filters and mini cupcake liners, or white paper, white string, and glue

DAY 15: CANDLELIGHT SINGING

Candle and lighter or flameless LED candles
Song lyrics if needed for your favorite hymns or Christmas carols

DAY 16: PLAY THE PLASTIC WRAP BALL GAME OR WRAP & DELIVER A GIFT

Roll of plastic wrap
Small prizes (coins, candies, fidget toys, mini toys, gift cards, etc.—anything that can be wrapped up into the ball that your family would enjoy)
Pair of dice
2 oven mitts for your hands
Note: *If you don't want to play the game, you can make or purchase a gift and wrap it to give to someone.*

DAY 17: BAKE & DELIVER HOLIDAY TREATS

Mini treat bags, cookie tubs, decorative paper plates and cling-wrap, cookie boxes, or zipper-top plastic bags to place cookies in
Gift tags and marker or pen to label gifts, if desired

DAY 18: SING CHRISTMAS CAROLS

Lyrics for your favorite Christmas carols, if needed
Mini Bluetooth speaker to connect to your phone to play Christmas carols if you need musical accompaniment (*be sure to build a playlist ahead of time*)
Other friends or family members to sing with you if you plan to go caroling door-to-door or in the community

Optional: mini candy canes to hand out at each house and invitations to your church's Christmas or Christmas Eve service, encouraging notes, or printables on the meaning of the candy cane (*from KatieJTrent.com/Advent*)

SECTION FOUR: LOVE

DAY 19: MAKE HANDPRINT WREATHS OR GIVE PROMISE RINGS

Green construction paper to place hands on and trace around
Glue or glue sticks
Scissors
Red construction paper to make holly berries, bows, etc.
Pen or marker to write promise verses (*if desired*)
Note: *Instead of doing the craft, you could choose to gift each of your kids with a promise ring as an outward expression of their love and commitment to Jesus. It could be any type of ring.*

DAY 20: MAKE HOLIDAY GIFTS

Treat bags or boxes for the peppermint bark (*or you could use zipper plastic bags*)
Paper to write notes (*or you can use the printable templates from KatieJTrent.com/Advent*)

DAY 21: SPREAD GENEROSITY

Give to a charity, write kind notes for people, serve in your community somewhere, help a neighbor, pay for a meal, put together blessing bags for the homeless, etc.
The blessing bags can be backpacks or gallon zipper bags. Fill them with warm hats, gloves, rain ponchos, scarves, mini shampoo bottles, conditioner, body wash, toothpaste, toothbrush, wipes, Q-tips, nail clippers, wash cloths, combs, hairbrushes, lo-

tion, disposable razors, protein bars, bottles of water, dried fruit, beef sticks, etc.

DAY 22: CHRISTMAS COLORING

Markers, crayons, or colored pencils
Christmas coloring pages (*or use the printable templates from Katie-JTrent.com/Advent*)
Blank white paper (*if you want to draw your own Christmas scenes to color*)

DAY 23: PLAY THE 3 GIFTS FOR JESUS GAME

Timer

DAY 24: TAKE COMMUNION TOGETHER

Unleavened bread (*from today's recipe*) or crackers/wafers
Grape juice or alternative (*or pre-packaged communion cups*)
Note: *If your family attends a Christmas Eve service today, you could take communion together there as well.*

DAY 25: PRAY & THANK JESUS

Nothing else is needed for today's activity, although you can snap a family photo with this book to share on social media how this Advent season has impacted your family. (*Please tag me @KatieJTrent and #KatieJTrentAdventures so I can rejoice and pray with you.*)

OPTIONAL GIFT
COUNTDOWN IDEAS

D oes your family use an Advent countdown calendar with little doors
that you open to reveal treats or figurines each day before Christmas? One of our family's Advent traditions involves unwrapping little gifts
each day from December 1 until Christmas Day.

These Advent gifts are small, inexpensive items you can purchase and
wrap ahead of time if you'd like a visual reminder of each day's theme as
you read *A Merry and Bright Adventure*. They consist of small tokens like
glow-in-the-dark stars, a birthday candle, an ornament, and an eraser.

If your family would like to try this, decide whether you will purchase
one item per day for the family to unwrap together or individual items for
each child to unwrap. Either way, you will number each wrapped gift from
twenty-four to zero you count down the days until Christmas.

Feel free to utilize your own ideas too. These are just suggestions, listed
by day. Write the number that is in parentheses on the Christmas tag to
help you unwrap the gifts in the right order:

December 1: (#24) An apple item *(eraser, keychain, figurine, etc.)*
December 2: (#23) Small, star-shaped item *(cookie cutter, key
chain, sticker, etc.)*
December 3: (#22) A coin *(use sharpie to black out one side)*; remind your kids that no matter how messy the coin is, it still has
value and purpose—and so do they

December 4: (#21) Christmas card, postage stamp, or pen

December 5: (#20) Red bow *(hair bow, bow tie, tiny gift wrap bow)*

December 6: (#19) Santa Claus *(hat, mini figure, etc.)*

December 7: (#18) Mini Christmas tree *(eraser, figurine, etc.)* or pine cone

December 8: (#17) Mini stocking with your child's name written on it

December 9: (#16) String of twinkling lights or mini flashlight

December 10: (#15) Mini candy cane

December 11: (#14) Written Christmas blessing for your family or a Bible verse *(like Numbers 6:24–26)* or something that says "Merry Christmas"

December 12: (#13) Poinsettia

December 13: (#12) Glow-in-the-dark stars

December 14: (#11) Angel

December 15: (#10) Mini LED candle

December 16: (#9) Mini wrapped present ornament or trinket

December 17: (#8) Baking item *(rolling pin, apron, chef hat, etc.)*

December 18: (#7) Music, song, or carol item

December 19: (#6) Ring or wreath

December 20: (#5) Small Bible or cross

December 21: (#4) Heart shaped item *(to go with the theme of generosity)*

December 22: (#3) Snow globe or something with the colors of Christmas

December 23: (#2) Wise men or gold, frankincense, or myrrh

December 24: (#1) Mini rolling pin, bread trinket, or another communion item

December 25: (#0-Christmas Day) Nativity set

ABOUT THE AUTHOR

Katie J. Trent is a respected leader in the Christian homeschool community and the founder of Family Faith-Building Academy. She has over a decade of experience in counseling children, teens, and families, having served as clinical director of two mental health agencies and as an elementary school counselor before transitioning to homeschooling and writing.

Along with her husband James, Katie also has more than fifteen years of ministry and church planting experience. In addition to *A Merry and Bright Adventure*, she authored *Recipes for a Sweet Child: Creative, Bible-Based Activities to Help Your Family Thrive* and *Dishing Up Devotions: 36 Faith-Building Activities for Homeschooling Families*.

Through writing, blogging, and speaking, Katie loves to equip and encourage strong, faith-filled families. She has been a featured speaker at many homeschool conferences and has written for the Upper Room, Crosswalk, *The Christian Journal* magazine, homeschooling and parenting blogs, and other ventures.

Katie received her B.A. in social work from Boise State University and her master's in social work from Northwest Nazarene University. She and James have a daughter and son, Kendra and Jordan.

Connect with Katie at KatieJTrent.com for more resources to help you put the fun back into the fundamentals of family discipleship.

More Family Faith-Building Resources

For more resources to grow your faith, strengthen your family, and simplify your homeschool, go to KatieJTrent.com. Katie shares information on giveaways, new resources, freebies, events, and product reviews.

Katie also invites you to join the Family Faith-Building Academy, a six-week digital course designed to equip Christian parents to effectively disciple their kids in fun, meaningful, and memorable ways. *(Groups such as co-ops, moms' groups, and churches can enroll at discounted rates.)* Learn more at FamilyFaithBuildingAcademy.com.

Searching for Community?

Katie created an online membership to connect with faith-filled families around the world! Move forward in your faith and family discipleship without confusion, frustration, or feeling overwhelmed. You'll find monthly themes to keep you focused, resources to equip and encourage you, fun virtual meetups, and more! Join free for thirty days at KatieJTrent.com/Community.

Practical Parenting Help

Katie's book *Recipes for a Sweet Child: Creative, Bible-Based Activities to Help Your Family Thrive* provides biblical solutions to thirty-six of the most common childhood struggles, including anger, anxiety, grief, tattling, sibling rivalry, resistance to schoolwork, peer pressure, and more. With devotions for parents, simple biblical lessons, discussion guides, fun family games and activities, and baking recipes as object lessons, this will become your go-to resource throughout your parenting journey.

Creative Character-Building

Katie's book *Dishing Up Devotions: 36 Faith-Building Activities for Homeschooling Families* offers thirty-six weekly activities to help your

256 *A Merry and Bright Adventure*

family build biblical character in fun and meaningful ways. Learn more at DishingUpDevotions.com.

Help Other Families

If you enjoy this book, you can make a huge difference by leaving an online review on Amazon, Goodreads, and other sites. Your quick review helps other families find this resource, and it also means a lot to Katie.

Join the Fun

Katie loves to see photos of families using and enjoying her resources. Please tag her @KatieJTrent and #KatieJTrentAdventures when sharing photos on social media so she can see and share the post.

Questions?

Katie is always happy to help however she can. Please email her anytime at Katie@KatieJTrent.com.